The
Non-Negotiable You
Mindset Mastery for Daily Success

Angie Wisdom

Published by 2 Market Media with Angie Wisdom.

ISBN 979-8-852-31454-3

I dedicate this book to my husband and two sons. Thank you for your grace and love through this amazing journey.

Shane — Thank you for telling me I need to find my "thing." Your passion for your own values changed my life. You will never know how much your unending support and belief in me means; I am truly the best version of myself with you.

Evan and Ethan, you two are my inspiration for showing up every day as the non-negotiable me. I pray I have shown you by example that you are capable of achieving your biggest and boldest dreams!

"*The Non-Negotiable You* is beautifully laid out and practical. Angie gives you tangible tools to create a morning mindset practice that impacts your life and compounds over time. As a leader, partner, and mother, starting my day grounded in a practice that honors myself first is the best thing I can do for everyone in my life because that little intentional effort reminds me that I can only show up for others when I've shown up for myself first."
Dom Farnan, *Chief Conscious Connector @ DotConnect, Author, Women in Business Advocate*

"Wow! I am in the business of empowerment, and the way Angie brings light to the many ways we can own our power to create the life we want is amazing. The principles she brings to the foundation of the Morning Mindset are a total game-changer."
Lizz Carter Clark, *International Speaker, National Best-Selling Author, Actress, and College Moxie Founder*

"In *The Non-Negotiable You*, Angie provides the step-by-step process to taking control of your day, your mindset, and your emotions. She provides an executable process and teaches you how to take back your power with fifteen simple minutes dedicated to YOU."
Stephani Cylmer, *Business Owner, Entrepreneur*

"*The Non-Negotiable You* is a must read. Angie's warmth and wisdom shine throughout this book as she guides us to create a life we love. Her Morning Mindset practice is pure gold. It can and will change your life. Ready to live your life to the fullest? This book will take you there!"
Diana Long, *MS, MCC, Speaker and Author*

"*The Non-Negotiable You* is a must read for anyone wanting to master themselves from the inside out and live their best life. The Morning Mindset has created invaluable growth and awareness!"
Tara Wilson, *Fierce Lab Founder, Podcast Host, Speaker and Entrepreneur of the Year*

"This is one of the best self-help books that I have ever read! It gives you detailed step by step actionable items to start your day with a win and truly live a life that you deserve!"
Israel Alayon, *CEO, Gemologist and Entrepreneur*

"Angie has a style and personable approach that makes you feel like she is speaking directly to you! In *The Non-Negotiable You*, she takes you on a journey of intuitive illuminating self-discovery that helps reveal your true values and self-awareness, that if used and practiced daily will bring you a happy and fulfilling life. I recommend *The Non-Negotiable You* to anyone who wants to live a life of greater meaning and fulfillment!
Melissa Robinson, *Senior Vice President, JW Cole*

CHAPTERS

INTRODUCTION

For twenty-five years, I've had the great fortune of taking a front-row seat in other people's lives, leading or coaching them through financial matters, life choices, and business decisions. I've learned that it's easy for people to want change, but not always simple for them to take action toward what they want. I've always wholeheartedly believed that people are capable of achieving whatever they want to pursue. They simply need to back action with the belief that they're capable and deserving! I've lived my life that way and tried my best to lead others to do the same.

My passion and desire to make an impact inspire me daily to help others create a path for the success they want. My experience and personal trials have proven that knowing yourself and putting yourself at the center of everything you do works. I didn't always operate from that perspective. For years I tried to succeed while working against myself and my own needs. I convinced myself that the only components to success were working harder and longer, sacrificing my personal values along the way. I couldn't have been more wrong, I was missing out on the most important piece to my potential: myself. Working with myself changed my life and career. The evidence lies in both my own success and joy and that of my clients. While you may not have the opportunity to sit down with me weekly as a private client, by reading this book, you're now part of my community. I can inspire you to start with yourself to create your best life ever.

Inspired by my experience, I created a practice called the Morning Mindset and saw the opportunity to bring a new way of living to my community that would help those who chose to embrace it. This book and this practice came from my own self-awareness and change, as well as from working with hundreds of clients and speaking to thousands of others, whether from the physical or virtual stage. I continually saw people facing different challenges, all originating from the same place: a lack of self mastery that comes from a relationship with oneself. I could see what was causing these recurring problems and challenges for people, which provided me with the opportunity to reverse engineer the struggles and create a proactive solution. As I brought the foundational pieces of the Morning Mindset to clients, I saw the change. Therefore, much of what you will read in the first six chapters of this book is as essential to creating your best life as the Morning Mindset practice itself. The *Start With You: Morning Mindset Journal* is a companion piece to this book. It's optional, though, as you can do the Morning Mindset in a journal of your own. The key is to do the practice every day, constantly developing a relationship with yourself, and as a result increasing your self mastery. The results you'll see are tantamount to those you would get from fancy coaching programs as long as you stay committed and honor your relationship with yourself. I did, and I still do today. Once I saw what I was capable of, I decided how I showed up for myself every day would be non-negotiable. It's why I have clarity every day about the life I want to live and how to create it. What I've created for you is an opportunity to take action and make a lifelong, sustainable change.

We get to create one life. If you're ready to create yours and live it to the fullest, you've found the right book. Commit now. You deserve all that this book will do for you.

1

YOU FIRST

Let's assume that today was an average day. You did what you needed to do, for the most part. You got work done, you followed through on most of your to-do list items, and while a few tasks slipped through the cracks, there's always tomorrow. Life is fine, maybe even good, but you have a feeling it could be better. It's not like you're miserable—far from it. You have a lot to be grateful for. In fact, you consider yourself happy, but not *really* happy. If you're honest with yourself, something is missing, and you have the desire to fix it but don't know how.

Here's the bottom line: Many people who are successful feel like they aren't tapping into all that they have to give. The days feel a little like a hamster wheel—they do what needs to be done, rinse, and repeat. If you're one of those people, you're frustrated because you've often thought there could be more. I don't mean more possessions, you've gone down that road. It never quite hits the mark, yet you keep setting your sights on another shiny object, hoping for a different result. Focusing on external wants won't get you where you want to go, I know this for a fact. The path lies within you. The "more" you're looking for happens when you start focusing on the most important piece of your success: *you.*

I've been in leadership roles for twenty plus years. I've led employees in one of the top financial institutions in the world, founded trading companies, and in my current coaching and consulting business, helped companies and individuals uncover the gaps and build the bridge to create the success they want. Each person has a distinct perspective and desire, yet the way to get there isn't so different. The challenges they face may differ, but the underlying problems are often similar. Underneath the surface desire or challenge, there's a need that consistently shows up that, when embraced, can change everything. This need gets overlooked and often taken for granted. It's a relationship with yourself that produces self mastery. Let's take a look at what could be contributing to this good, but not best, life:

- You think you are in your own way. You have so much noise in your head that it's hard to find a moment of peace, let alone clarity.
- You don't take time for yourself and what matters most to you, leaving you drained and exhausted.
- You don't prioritize commitments to yourself, everyone and everything else is more important.
- You break promises to yourself, making it hard to lead from a place of trust.
- You worry about other people's opinions and feelings, which has you second-guessing your authenticity.
- You keep trying to find happiness in a prize or finish line, all the while missing the joy that's right in front of you.
- You know what you "need" to do, but it's still not getting done.
- You want something to change, but excuses are abundant and you aren't taking responsibility to make it happen.

- You know you haven't given your blood, sweat, and tears to what you really want, and that feeling sucks.
- You get a fresh start every day, but you aren't being intentional about creating it the way you want.

If you can relate to this list, I understand. I once did too. And what's crazy is you can be moderately successful in spite of everything I listed.

So, what do you want to do about it? Two pages into the book and I'm already asking you questions that are likely making you uncomfortable. Fair warning: my clients say I listen like a mom but deliver like a dad; you need that awareness and honesty to make the changes you want. Here's the best news: Everything I just mentioned above that feels out of control, every piece is actually *in* your control. Yes, it is all in your control! I'll never ask you to focus on something that's out of your control, it's a waste of time and energy. When you work on self mastery you have the power to consciously execute change. This isn't about anyone else, only you have the ability to change the harsh reality I just laid out. You don't have to live that way, but you must choose to take the power to execute change. All the noise, stories, thoughts, and feelings in your head make it hard to have any room for yourself—this has to change in order to tap into your full potential. It happens as soon as you adjust your life to start with yourself first! Creating space to be in control of your mindset will take some time. Right now, you let yourself slide instead of holding yourself accountable for your day and being the best version of yourself. I know, I've been where you are. It can be deceiving, since so far, you've gotten away with "succeeding" without what I'm teaching you. It's easier and more comfortable to stay where we are, when you don't "have" to change. But take it from me, if you are a person who won't be satisfied until you've truly tapped into what you are capable of; you need what I'm laying out for you.

How do we begin? We work on building a foundation, starting with your values and creating a relationship with yourself. Since you're ambitious, you've no doubt tried endless tactics to see if you could really tap into your unleashed potential, but my guess is that you've been trying specific tips and tricks—in other words, shortcuts. Reading the latest book on how to increase productivity, manage your time, or create better habits can be effective pieces that you'll use eventually, but those are only as good as the person implementing them. This is a different route, one that works because it starts with you!

Moving toward this new state of being is going to take creating an awareness that will open the door to new choices and change. The major reason you're in your own way is a lack of consistent awareness. You may have clarity one day, but it's fleeting, and that's because it's not truly focused on you. Oftentimes you're problem solving for the life that you're currently in, not the life you want to lead.

Awareness is in thoughts and feelings. You're simply going to take notice on a day-to-day basis of what you're thinking and feeling about your current life so you can become empowered to do something about it. Your awareness will grow once you accept it as an opportunity instead of a judgment. In that space, you'll learn how to be present in the moment, ditching worry and fear and finding true joy.

Your values are part of this awareness practice. Values have to be explored and reviewed so you can give yourself what matters to you daily. If not, you'll keep producing at the level you are. We're a society driven by giving, but we often don't refuel or give to ourselves, which ironically can produce some of the most valuable successes. We get off on how much we produce and how hard we work and how we show up for others, but we're ignoring ourselves in the process. We get a prize for hitting our redline and emptying our tank, but we ultimately lose. There's a better way.

If you go against the grain and start with yourself and awareness of your values, life changes for the better. In the present moment, with this newly-created awareness, you'll find a quieter state of being because you're aligned with your personal integrity. Initially, this feels uncomfortable. What happened to all the busyness and doing? Soon you can start using this space to create the life you want. You aren't running on the hamster wheel anymore. Life becomes more intentional because you're creating it. You'll learn to consciously control your mind, stepping out of what's next and staying in the present moment. Here you're giving yourself a chance to sit with yourself. Having your values in mind guides your intentions. You can accomplish your big goals and continue to buy your fancy things, but if you don't know how to be present, you'll be empty and massively confused by the lost feeling you have later.

Through this process, you form a new, honest relationship with yourself, where you can be authentic and guide yourself away from what doesn't serve you and toward your best life. It's a little scary any time you form a new relationship, but it's exciting at the same time. You'll have to look at the way you operate (even when you'd rather not) and embrace the idea that ignorance is not bliss. This truth will set you free. If the thought of self-discovery causes a deep inhale, that's a good sign that you're on the right track.

The way to reach this new you isn't an overnight fix, but a methodical daily fifteen minute process I call the Morning Mindset. I have taken hundreds of clients directly through the Morning Mindset, and thousands of others have embraced this practice too. It works. But if you want a relationship with yourself that allows you to create meaningful success and a life you love, you have to trust the process. Isn't that worth ten or fifteen minutes a day? You can't compare this to something else that you've tried and failed. I'm not asking you to master time management or productivity, I'm asking you to put yourself first and be your best guide. You can do that.

Here's the deal, though. You can't just jump into the Morning Mindset. Trying to jump straight in would be no better than chasing the next quick-fix strategy. You need to understand how to get out of your way before you can have the space to create your day and, ultimately, your best life. Some of you might be tempted to jump to Chapter Eight where I explain the Morning Mindset, but it's best not to rush. The journey you have ahead of you is about creating your best life; it's worth taking your time to get there. Take the time in Chapters Two through Seven to understand yourself. Only then will you understand what the non-negotiable version of you is capable of. Then the Morning Mindset will make so much sense. You can have meaningful success and a life you love if you're willing to give yourself the time to create every morning. You are the key component to all you want. I know that sounds obvious, but so many people point their focus outward instead of inward when it comes to creating a life beyond their wildest dreams. The insights I'm going to teach you will require you to do the work. No more quick fixes and bursts of motivation. The changes will be lifelong and sustainable, and you're going to operate as a different person. Get ready to leave behind the heaviness that's been weighing you down. You're always the most important piece of the equation, so it only makes sense that the work to do is on yourself. You are the producer of your meaningful success, the creator of your best life. It all starts with you!

In my former career as an investment advisor, I looked successful and on top of the world. I was working hard and was grateful for all that I had. I helped clients that I loved, and I was good at it. Then I moved into management and coached other advisors. By the age of 24, I was hitting all my goals. I had a great marriage, and we were already on our way to building substantial wealth. I liked my work, but it felt like every single day was the same. I couldn't stop thinking that there had to be more. Every time the thought popped up, I would shut it down: "All is good, Angie! Stop overthinking, be grateful." Yet, I still felt like something was missing. I looked over the boxes I was supposed to be checking. Check, check, check—they were all there. I was doing what I "needed" to do, but I wasn't looking beyond the surface of what I was supposed to be doing. I needed a different level of awareness, more presence, and control over my mind. I didn't have a relationship with myself that allowed me to be honest and aware. The lack of an authentic connection with myself prevented me from digging to find the real answers and kept me on the hamster wheel and limited my success and joy. Why? Because it's really hard to be truthful with yourself. We lie to ourselves every day. It's less painful than knowing the truth. We're the only ones who know we're lying, so it's easy to get away with it. That lack of an honest and aware relationship with myself kept me from knowing what possibilities I had or what I could be inspired to do. I needed to start a relationship that went beyond checking the daily boxes and thinking my life was complete. One where I could create a deeper awareness and listen to what I wanted and valued. I was tired of the status quo and wanted to see what I had in me. I sought excitement about creating my life. I wanted to be inspired, and I wanted my mind to think about limitless possibilities instead of the typical BS that takes up residence in our minds. I wanted to be more in control of what I thought about.

As I considered these new life changes, I decided to see what would happen if I built that relationship with myself. I had built other companies and relationships in which I played a major role. What if, in addition to always helping and leading others, I started doing the same for myself? I would commit to allocating dedicated time and mental capacity to myself like I gave to others. I would start taking responsibility for what brought me deep joy. I knew I was capable of more, so I would figure out a way to tap into that. I would start working with myself to create the best version of myself and the life I wanted. No one else was going to do it; it started with me. The journey to master myself and tap into my full potential was non-negotiable.

The time I allocated to myself and my values led to honesty and awareness that I hadn't experienced before. I created a new operating system built from what I did and didn't like. I got honest with how I was truly feeling and what I wanted to change. I realized that I was in control to make any change I wanted, I didn't have to get stuck being a victim. I had the power, I just had to be aware and use it. What could I do if I took responsibility for my own day? If I decided what I wanted to create? What if I tapped into my mind every morning to make all these choices around what mattered most to me? All these pieces started to come together, and in that moment, I knew that if I wanted to create meaningful success and a life I loved, I was going to have to create it myself every single day. That was the answer. No more waiting to see what my day would give me, I was going to decide what I wanted in my day. I didn't want to wake up to cross another day off my calendar until vacation showed up; I wanted to jump out of bed excited about my day and new opportunities. I didn't want to just do the job I was supposed to do and win the award, I wanted to surprise myself and do more than I ever thought I was capable of. I didn't want to rely upon other people throughout the day to make me feel valuable, I wanted to feel valuable before I even faced the day. It was time to get in the driver's seat and take control. I knew that to find out what I was truly capable of, I had to create that awareness myself. My true happiness depended on me knowing how. I started a variation of the Morning Mindset that I share in this book, and I never looked back. Take a minute and assess your life right now:

Rate the qualities below on a scale of 1-10 (1 being lowest and 10 the highest)

- Your relationship with yourself
- Your ability to know what fills you with joy or gives you meaning
- Your commitment to spending time every day listening to yourself
- Your ability to self assess, check in to see how you are and what you need
- How honest are you with yourself
- Keeping commitments you make with yourself
- Holding yourself accountable
- Your ability to take action to create the life you want every day

It's okay if your assessments are coming in lower than you like, that's the honesty and awareness you need to make a change. The path we'll walk together will help you course-correct. In the past, maybe you did well with hard work, grit, sacrifice, perseverance, and determination, but we're going to add a special ingredient that's going to take you to the next level. You've gotten by, but it's okay to admit that it's not enough to truly love the life you're living. It's time to step it up and look inward. Learn what you value, make choices that serve you, live in the present, and take responsibility for what you want in your life. Creating that life you love starts with you first, today, and every day going forward, is a non-negotiable. Before you tune in to what other people need from you, or what might be going on in the world, give yourself time to prepare for your most important role: creating happiness and success for *yourself*.

Embracing this new role is going to require a shift in perspective. You need to start your day thinking about yourself and what you want. If you just cringed at that thought, let me tell you: first, you do have the time, and second, yes, it makes a bigger impact than you can imagine right now. Whatever else you're currently putting first will have to take second place. I can assure you that you'll be better for it, and those around you will also benefit. I'm telling you from personal experience and the experiences of my clients, you'll show up so much better if you check in with yourself first before you start your day. You'll be operating from a full tank, and you'll have more patience, compassion, and confidence. You'll also have better mental and physical health, less stress, and much more. You'll be adding real value to your relationships. Goodbye stressed-out, resentful, and exhausted you. Hello, joyful, authentic, energetic, and confident you! You'll see that putting yourself first makes you a better human for yourself and everyone around you. Decide now to have an open mind and put yourself first.

To further explain, when I say that meaningful success and living your best life are first and foremost, I define this in a few different ways:

- Spending time with yourself and creating the life you want first thing in the morning is key to showing up as your best self for others.

- Defining and putting your values first adjusts how authentically you show up for your life and make decisions.
- Gaining control of your mind and working from a new perspective is key before you look on the outside.
- Working and living from a you-first perspective is going to give you the best relationship with yourself.

What this all comes down to is mastering a state of mind control, authenticity, and presence. You're going to know yourself better than ever before. You'll see your authentic, genuine self more and more every day, and that's exciting! You'll know exactly what you need and when you need it. The relationship you create with yourself will be life changing. People will be attracted to you, not because you bend yourself into a pretzel for them, but because you have a sense of confidence and calm about you.

The path I'll take you on is ultimately one of reprogramming and rewiring. You've given way too much mental energy and space to other people's thoughts. You've been making decisions based on feelings instead of what you value. You've moved so fast that you haven't enjoyed the present and worry about what's next all the time. Other people's priorities get in the way of what you want, so you exist like a victim instead of taking responsibility. All of this gets in the way of you being your best self and creating your best life. This is the junk we're going to let go of and the thinking we're going to rewire.

To create your best life every day, you'll need to be committed and consistent with your intentions and what you want to create. You'll have to be confident in your authentic self and not care about what others think. You'll need to live in the moment and be grateful for what you experience. And you must take full responsibility for the life and success you want. No more waiting, you'll be creating! You might be thinking that this sounds amazing, but that it also sounds like a lot of work. It's a lot of *change*, not a lot of work.

With the Morning Mindset, you're working on the "who" pieces, which help you understand yourself and your priorities. You'll methodically set goals, work through your values, tap into new awareness, set intentions, make affirmations, and incorporate gratitude, prayer, and visualization. The Morning Mindset consists of these key pieces, which I'm going to lead you through in the upcoming chapters so you'll know how to most effectively execute it in Chapter Eight.

At the end of the day in your Daily Reflection, you'll hold yourself accountable by looking at your values and intentions to see if they showed up. At the bare minimum, you'll be building habits of commitment, consistency, awareness, and a positive mindset. At the next level, you'll be creating that priceless relationship with yourself. But first, we need the "who" handled. People try to shortcut the "who" and get straight to the "what" before they're fully aware of what they're truly capable of in a life aligned with their values. The shortcuts don't give you the ultimate result. They may help you handle one decision on a Tuesday, but they aren't sustainable if the ultimate aim is to change your life. You have to do the work on yourself first (see, there it is again, you first). You are the producer of all your results, so to be in the optimal position to execute top skills and endeavors, you need to be in a consistent, committed, responsible, honest, aware, proactive, and present mindset to make the best choices. The Morning Mindset gives you the highest level of capability. I'm so excited to prepare you for what will become second nature yet radically change your life and leave you inspired to create greatness.

If what I'm saying is resonating with you or making you feel uncomfortable, maybe even a little angry with me, then we're on the right track! There's a different way, and it's not monumental. I've done the work of learning the concepts in the Morning Mindset, and I use it with all my clients. I do the Morning Mindset every morning and I reflect daily. I live it. I coach people through it every day! Much of it is simple to understand, but not always easy to do. Sustainable change is never easy. You have to work for it, but I promise it's worth it.

Fast-forward to several months from now. You've done the Morning Mindset every day. Here's a snapshot of the potential new you:

In the morning, you wake up excited to start your day because you're in control of what it looks like. You have time to create the new version of success that you now feel confident you can achieve. You're laughing and living in the present moment because you no longer worry about the future. You feel fulfilled and confident with ending your day because you know you put your best effort in. You're showing up authentically because you don't care what other people think; you now trust that they can handle their own shit because you know how to handle yours.

Did you notice the common word in all those statements? *You!* Pretty different from the original list, right?

What would you do with this new trust in yourself, this new love for yourself, the new respect and boundaries you have for yourself? I don't expect you to know all those answers this soon, and I bet some of that imagery doesn't seem possible, but I assure you that by the time you put this book down, you'll be teaching this practice to your friends, trying to get people on board because it's been such a gamechanger for you. After years of learning and education and coaching and personal development, I learned that we all hold the power to create whatever we want in our life. I know it sounds a little cliché, but really, it's true. You just have to choose to take action and take responsibility for it.

If you're choosing yes, then our first step to starting with you is to work around your values. You can't live your best life without knowing and living your values. So many people don't know what their values are or have let them slide out of the picture because they don't conform to the schedules or choices of the people around them. Without a clear examination of your values, you make choices and decisions that are disconnected from the true you. Once you understand and connect with your values, you'll have a new kind of awareness about yourself. You'll understand the importance of your own personal value. You'll open the door to building a life that once felt unattainable and now is a tangible possibility.

2

YOUR VALUES

Values are the foundation of what's most important to you, and they show up in all that you do: the way you find joy, every decision you make, and every goal you set. If you aren't living a value-aligned life, you're missing out on what's most important to you. It's that deprivation that creates a lack of happiness no matter how much you have. Your values are the compass that guides your life, beliefs, and actions. If you don't know your values, what's guiding your thoughts, decisions, and behavior? Without that guide, you'll feel lost, stuck, unhappy, burnt out, and even depressed. Starting with you means finding the values that will lead you to your best life and most meaningful success.

One of my clients named Eric made a confession to me during his first session.

"Angie, I have everything I've ever wanted. I have a beautiful family, an amazing home, great friends, and my business is better than ever. I have fifteen employees and we exceed our revenue goals year after year, so I should be the happiest man on earth . . . but I'm not. What's wrong with me? I'm grateful and blessed beyond belief, but I feel horrible admitting that I still feel like something is missing."

I could hear the guilt and shame in his voice.

"Eric, what do you value in life?" I asked.

"My family, my health, my friends, financial stability."

"What brings you joy on a daily basis?"

"I love seeing my kids and wife happy. I like seeing the business do well and I like providing for my employees."

"What do you do for yourself that brings you joy?"

He took a long pause before he answered.

"I don't have a lot of extra time. Business has been so busy. The kids have so much going on. We're always going. It's nice when we get away for a vacation, but it's been a while."

Eric's story was a classic. Life had taken over, and he was missing out on some of the values that would fill him up. He didn't even know what all of his values were.

"Take me back to when life was less busy, maybe before work took off or before the kids had a busy schedule," I instructed him. "Think back to when you had more time. How were you spending it? What were those moments that made you feel great?"

"Oh man, that was a long time ago. I used to go mountain biking. I loved being out there on my own, it was so peaceful. I didn't have anything on my mind except focusing on the trail and making it up the hills. I always felt great afterward, like I'd earned my time to relax. I used to read more too. When I was focused on growing my business, I would read all the time, trying to learn how I could get an edge. It made me feel like I was always growing and in the know. When the kids were younger, we could just spend a day at the beach or hang out in the park. Back then I actually got to play with them and laugh with them."

I smiled watching him reflect on one joyful memory after another. He was watching the old videos of his life and reliving them with a big smile every time he thought of another moment. He focused on me again.

"I need to get back on my bike. I have to start reading again. I have to do something to quiet my mind and get some peace."

"It sounds like you just remembered a few important values of yours that haven't been showing up. What are you learning?"

"I need to be challenged physically, like riding. I also need to be learning. And I need some time alone to get a clear, peaceful mind."

Getting Eric to think about the times he felt great allowed him to uncover what brings him joy. As we dug deeper into the memories, we were able to frame what that joy represented in the form of values. In addition to what he was already confident of—financial security, health, family, friends—he discovered that quality time with family, alone time, peace and tranquility, accomplishment, and personal growth were also vital to his own personal happiness. He had forgotten to put the attention on himself, instead making his values whatever made everyone else happy.

What Eric was experiencing isn't uncommon. I see it all the time. It's one of the first conversations I have with clients. What do you do for *you?* What makes you happy? What fills your cup? I see the transition happen really quickly. They see that what they used to love isn't showing up anymore. Life changed, and at some point, those values they once cherished and gave focus to got put on the back burner or tossed to the side. They decided there wasn't room for what they needed and that family, work, and other responsibilities were more important.

You cannot live your best life without your values.

I would say that you are likely in one of two camps: *A*, you don't know what your values are, or at least you don't know all of them, especially the ones that pertain only to yourself. Or *B*, you think you know your values and that you're living a value-aligned life, but you might be selling yourself a story, basing your values on what shows up in your life every day. You think you value a busy schedule, challenges, and a lot of social contact. The tell-tale sign that this needs a second look is that you still aren't completely filled up. You can fall into a lack of honesty because knowing the truth would hurt. When you really unpack what's showing up in your day and ask how a busy schedule makes you feel, you may reveal that you're exhausted and just want to hide from it all. The truth is the values you think you have aren't cup-fillers, they're time-takers.

Regardless of how you ended up in a place of not knowing your values or not living a value-aligned life, it has to change. You cannot live your best life and create meaningful success without your values. I'm not teaching you something you've never known. At some point, even if it was a long time ago, your values guided you, even if you didn't know it. You engaged in the activities that filled you up. You made choices based on what was most important to you. But life happened, and somewhere along the way, your values were sacrificed. You started adulting and thought you couldn't afford to take time for what used to feel so important to you. Like Eric, the company you're trying to build needs all of you. Or the promotion you're working so hard to earn requires you to sacrifice everything right now. Or your family comes first, so you go without. These thoughts are exactly what have you tossing your values to the side and starving yourself of joy, excitement, energy, and motivation. The real truth is that you can't afford *not* to live a value-aligned life. Ditching your values might get you the job, build your company, make your family happy—all temporary fixes and highs—but it will come full circle eventually, and you'll be left to deal with the devastation. The resentment, the lack of motivation, the vices to numb the empty feeling, the lack of patience, lack of energy, lack of compassion, and just not giving a crap.

The alternative, if you're willing to start the work on yourself, is to be aware of your true values and start living a value-aligned life. The result is joy, energy, excitement, motivation, creation, patience, compassion, and empowerment. I'd say those are pretty powerful reasons for your values to be part of the non-negotiable you. I live a value-aligned life, and I help hundreds of people each year do the same, which is how I know it works. I've witnessed countless breakthroughs when people realize that it starts with themselves and their values. Living a value-aligned life makes you a better person for you and everyone around you. That company you're building has more meaning and you're leading from a full tank. That promotion comes easier because you can execute with a clearer mind and remain energized and motivated. The family you're giving your time to loves your patience, compassion, presence, and energy. You living your values creates a net gain in productivity and time. You'll become more efficient when it's worth it for you. Your values, the most important compass in your life, are worth it. You are worth it!

You might be thinking, "Sure, sounds great, but how am I supposed to do that with all of these other obligations? I work, I have a family, I have a company..." I get it, but you can still get your values in, I promise. Living a value-aligned life just takes some creativity and modification. The way you used to see your values show up before the big company, family, and social calendar was probably a little different. My client Eric may not get to go mountain biking for hours every day, but he certainly doesn't have to neglect it altogether. Getting your values in daily doesn't take an all-or-nothing approach. Just because you can't have an entire hour of peaceful alone time doesn't mean you stomp your feet and say, "What's the point? I might as well not do it at all." Wrong! Take what you can, even if it's ten minutes. When you give yourself what matters most, you send yourself a message that you matter! That message creates confidence. That ten minutes you put into your value has worth beyond the ten minutes, so trust me here. You can modify, and I'll show you how. But first, let's uncover those values.

How do you find out what your values are? There are three ways for you to explore what your five to seven core values are: discovery, memories/reflection, and daily awareness.

For discovery, ask yourself these few questions, and you'll likely uncover some obvious values:

1. What makes you feel great? There isn't a right or wrong answer. Some common ones that come up are exercise, alone time, eating healthy, and spending time with friends or family.
2. When do you feel energized? Is it when you are engaging with others, accomplishing difficult things, being creative, or competing at something?
3. What's the most important thing you need to see in your life? Connection with others? Throwing events or parties? They can be specific, or they may be more general, like stability and security, change and variety, financial freedom, time freedom, peace, or spirituality.

Answering questions like these bring up the top-of-mind answers you're most aware of and probably work to have in your life. These more obvious values are good, write them down. But there are almost always other values that you aren't aware of and that take a bit more digging to uncover.

For reflection/memories, let's take you down memory lane for a minute to discover the best memories and most joyful moments that hold your values. Think back to the last time you were overjoyed, the last memory that puts a big smile on your face, maybe even gives you butterflies or goosebumps thinking about it. Got it?

Now explore it, what made it so great?

1. Where were you? In nature, in your home, at a friend's house, traveling, in school, at work, in church?
2. Who were you with? Family, friends, coworkers, alone, with new people?
3. What were you doing? Learning, being in service, socializing, competing, accomplishing, relaxing, being creative?
4. What emotion did it create? Peaceful, busy, connected, capable, competent, at ease, knowledgeable?

The memory itself may be a specific experience, but the answers to the questions about the experience will reveal your values.

Add these values to your list.

The third part— daily awareness— will uncover the values you might not even know fill you up. Ask yourself this simple question every evening: What brought me joy today? This question is going to help you uncover any less obvious values. You'll either get confirmation of the values you already know, or you might uncover something new to explore. Don't panic if you come up with nothing, that's normal if you haven't been giving yourself what you need. Just be honest so you have the space to grow. Keep asking and reflecting. Eventually, you'll find yourself writing down an activity or action that aligns with your values, like a workout if you value physical activity, or maybe landing a new client if you value accomplishment. When you write something down that's not already on the values list, consider adding it.

Every once in a while, you might write something down that makes you stop and think. I recently wrote down making dinner. Not an obvious answer for me, but when I thought about it, I saw that cooking and bringing my family together for a meal brought me joy. I also realized that I felt accomplished; I hadn't cooked for a while because of my schedule, but when I did, I felt really good about it. That doesn't mean I need to cook every night, but getting something in that makes me feel accomplished is important to me.

Your fondest memories reveal your values.

I was giving a keynote on living a value-aligned life to female financial advisors, and I asked them to think back to the last time they were overjoyed. Some of them looked like they hadn't been asked that question in a long time. One of the women spoke up: "One of my most recent great memories was on vacation with my family. We were hiking and mountain biking."

I could tell she was doubting that her values were hiking and mountain biking. I knew they weren't, but we were on the path to finding her values.

"What was great about these experiences?" I asked her.

"The bike ride was fun. I had an electric bike, so for once, I was able to keep up with my husband. I wouldn't have been able to do the ride without the electric bike. And the hike, it was exciting to get to the top and conquer the mountain."

"How did these experiences make you feel?"

"Proud, capable, and accomplished."

I saw the light bulb go off in her head, and her eyes grew brighter. She continued sharing what was coming up for her and what she was discovering.

"I just realized how important it is to me to feel capable and competent. I also love accomplishment and conquering challenges."

She had just added two core values to her list, (1) feeling capable and competent and (2) accomplishment. The values she had discovered didn't have to wait until she was on vacation. She could bring them into her life daily. She thought about her work and how she could take certain actions with her clients to get that feeling of being capable and accomplished every day.

Sometimes it's difficult to recall that last joyful memory, especially for people-pleasers who tend to make everyone else's happiness a priority. So you might have to go back in time, way back. Your fondest memories reveal your values. Don't be discouraged, I promise the memory is in there if you're willing to look for it.

Recently a client of mine said, "I can't even remember the last time I was that happy and full of joy."

We waited for a minute as she went all the way back to college when she was in performing arts. She was onstage, singing and dancing, being the center of attention.

"I think the time has passed for me to get back onstage, so what am I supposed to do?" she asked with defeat.

As I asked detailed questions about how she felt in those moments while performing and what was so joyful about those experiences, she realized she was energized when she was in the spotlight.

"I loved expressing myself in a creative way and being recognized and acknowledged," she confessed.

These values were important to her, and she got all of them when she was performing. She could find ways to get those values now, ways she can be in the spotlight, express her creativity, and be acknowledged. Together we explored what that would look like in her life now.

I'll teach you how to do that once we have your list of core values.

Finding your values is a process of self-exploration. It doesn't always come easily because society has taught us to ignore what we need and tend to others. I'm a giver and a server, but I'm at my best when I've given and served myself first. You have to trust this to start leaning into your values. When I take my group program clients through this process, they discover their values, and then I tell them to start living them immediately. Their job is to experience those values and come back and let me know what it was like. My clients go away scared, nervous, and excited all at the same time. They don't know how it's going to happen, but they're determined to give it their best for that next week. Without fail, they come back the next week shocked.

"I can't believe the difference it makes!" they tell me. "I was so much more productive. I had more patience. I was less stressed and more focused. I was excited to wake up and start my day."

"Yes, because you're fueling yourself. You can't run on empty!"

The time you take for yourself pays you back ten times over. So lean in, don't judge, just explore and create awareness by asking yourself the questions I just taught you.

After you've tried the three ways to extract your values—discovery, memories/reflection, and daily awareness—look at your list. Don't worry about it being perfect. You'll reflect and grow with it when we get to the Morning Mindset. Do your best to narrow your list down to five to seven values. Here are some sample values that might help you fine-tune your list:

- Balanced life
- Time freedom
- Financial freedom
- Spiritual way of life
- Alone time

- Socialization
- Peace
- Accomplishment
- Challenge
- Creativity
- Acknowledgment
- Competence
- Personal growth
- Family time
- Time in nature
- Contributing to society
- Mental stimulation

You can put anything on the list beyond my suggestions, so trust yourself to name them so we can start defining your unique values. You can use my value assessment to help you decide what values are most important to you. Scan the QR code at the end of the chapter.

It's your responsibility to get your values to show up.

If finding your values is the first step, then understanding what they look like in your life is the second step. You can't go after something you haven't defined. If you say you value financial freedom, you must define what that looks like before you can take any real action toward living a life of financial freedom. This is true for any of your values. If you value peace and tranquility, what does that look like in your life? How do you experience tranquility? Your answer is going to be different than someone else's.

Peace and tranquility happen to be a value of mine, and for me, I live in peace and tranquility by not letting my emotions take over. I grew up in a home where yelling was common, so peace and tranquility mean no yelling. I know what it looks like, so I can make the right choices every day to live in peace and tranquility.

I was speaking at another event when a woman said, "Peace and tranquility is a value of mine, but I don't know how to get it. I have four kids, and my husband and I both work."

"What makes you feel like you don't have peace and tranquility?" I asked.

"Coming home from work and having to make another twenty decisions for the rest of the family. What's for dinner? What show are the kids watching? Who can go outside and play? What should we do tonight? One decision after another."

"Okay, so what would give you peace and tranquility?"

"Not making so many decisions after work!"

I saw the excitement in her eyes when the clarity hit her. I didn't need to say anything more.

"I'm going to ask my husband if he can make some of these decisions instead. I'm going to decide what's for dinner early in the week so I don't have to decide that night. I'm going to ask the kids to check with their dad for decisions. I just never knew that's what was causing me unrest."

Her definition of peace and tranquility is much different than mine. Without defining it, she would've never been able to take action to achieve it. She thought it was impossible to have peace with both parents working and raising four kids, but once she understood what peace in her life could look like, she could begin to work toward that goal. You have to do the same thing. Take your list of values, and for each one, ask, "What would this look like for me in my life?" Write out your answers. Some will be easier to define than others. For me, time freedom looks like putting my phone away in the evening so I'm not checking my emails. A balanced life looks like having time to work out in the morning. Financial freedom looks like allocating funds to my IRA and not spending excessively. In contrast, some of the other values you discover may need more thought and exploration.

It's your responsibility to get your values to show up. I used to be a gymnast when I was in high school and I always felt amazing when I was competing. I felt accomplished and capable every time I practiced and performed. I was about twenty-six when I decided I would try gymnastics again. It was short-lived, but I went back to try again around twenty-nine and one last time around thirty-two. It became a joke in my house. My husband would say, "You aren't going back to gymnastics again, are you?" I didn't realize at the time that I was trying to get the values of feeling accomplished and capable back into my life. I had lost them when I started my career, got married, and had kids. I focused so much of my time on everyone else that I didn't know what values were most important to me. I just knew that being a gymnast was a great time in my life, and I was searching for that fulfillment again, trying to put an old life into a new container. Once I knew what the values were that I was seeking, I could start taking action to put them in my life in a way that fit who I'd become. It may not be competing on a gymnastic floor, but I could still compete in other areas of my life and feel competent and accomplished. I started to play golf to fill the values of competing and feeling capable and accomplished.

Be open to exploring what your old values could look like in your current life. I'm going to remind you again that your discovery may not be perfect the first time. You may try to play classical piano three more times before you realize you want to play drums. It's not a one-and-done process. You'll always be trying and reflecting on what fills you up. So don't get stuck trying to make it perfect, define it and give it a go. In the Morning Mindset, you'll have the opportunity to reflect and make changes.

If you are following along with me, you should now have a list of your values and how they can be experienced in your life going forward. Your list may look like this:

- Alone time—twenty minutes in the morning for my morning routine, reading, and prayer
- Physical activity—climbing class, going for a walk, or Peloton

- Capable and competent—doing my Morning Mindset routine, working with clients
- Peace and tranquility—pausing before I respond, keeping my emotions in check
- Personal growth—reading time in the morning
- Spirituality—daily devotional
- Family time—foosball, ping-pong, or time to talk

You can use my Values in Action worksheet to list and define what your values look like to you. Scan the QR code at the end of the chapter.

Congratulations! You have a list of values and ideas for taking action toward them. Now it's time to start living a value-aligned life. A value-aligned life is one where you're intentional about living a life based on what's most important to you by making choices that align with your values and setting goals based on achieving them.

Make your decisions based on values, not feelings.

In a value-aligned life, your values act as fuel. You need to consume them to stay fulfilled and energized. Think of yourself as having battery capacity. When you take time to get your values in, you're charging your battery. If you have alone time, your battery goes up 15 percent. If you get to be creative, your battery charges another 15 percent. If you get your family time in, your battery charges another 15 percent. When you take responsibility for keeping your battery charged, you stay energized and able to perform, you can give to others, and you're more present. If you neglect to charge your battery, you'll be drained, and giving to others will feel like a chore. You'll be less patient, not present, and exhausted. It's your life, and it's your job to get your values to show up. Remember, you already know what they are and what they could look like in your life, so now it's about taking action to put them there.

Making decisions based on your values is another piece of living a value-aligned life. The majority of the time, people make decisions based on how they feel in the moment. It's a default way of making decisions, and it's also a crapshoot. Your feelings are fleeting, they change all the time based on your energy, your environment, your circumstances. Translation: the decision you make based on your feelings one minute might be one you regret in ten minutes. I'm sure you can think back to the last time you said, "Why did I agree to this? How did I end up here?" Those are decisions you made based on feelings. Oftentimes they're not even your feelings, but rather someone else's feelings. You didn't want them to be mad or upset with you, so you made the decision to go along with them, even if it encroached on time for your values. Repeatedly making decisions based on feelings can make you dread decisions because you don't trust yourself. You think, "Should I or shouldn't I? I remember what happened last time. I don't want to regret this!" The good news is, there's no more regret if you start making decisions based on your values.

Your values are what's most important to you, they don't change every day. You don't value financial freedom on Monday but not on Tuesday. Your values are constant, which means your decisions are based on something that won't change in five minutes. The non-negotiable you makes your decisions based on your values, not feelings.

Here's a common example of making a choice based on feelings: You value physical activity and a healthy lifestyle. Your alarm goes off to get up for a workout, but you feel tired and decide to sleep in. That's a feeling-based decision. Hours later, you're kicking yourself because you didn't stick to what's important to you, and you're regretful. That regret might produce more regrettable action: "Well, I already missed my workout, my day is shot, so I might as well eat the cake too."

Here's how the same scenario would look with a value-based decision: The alarm goes off, you feel tired, but you know how important your exercise is to you. You're going to choose your value because you know how good you'll feel about it later. No regrets.

Make sure what you want to create aligns with your values.

The final piece of living a value-aligned life is making sure that what you're creating aligns with your values. As I've said before, you are the creator of your joy and your success. You get to make the choices and have the responsibility for creating what you want. If you don't set your vision and goals based on your values, you'll end up achieving something you thought you wanted but didn't in the end. That might seem like a no-brainer, but trust me, you'd be surprised how many people set goals and create a future vision without their values in mind.

My client Mike was fed up with his boss. He didn't like the way his boss managed the business, and he was tired of giving up a large portion of his income to the company for what he felt wasn't worth it. He decided to start his own company, run it differently, treat his employees better, and make a lot more money. He did. And then he came to me because he wanted to figure out how to get out of this position.

"I never wanted to manage people. I never wanted to deal with all the company bullshit. I'm tired of hearing everyone's problems, I just want to go back to doing my own thing, helping clients, and being done at the end of the day," he said with frustration.

I started asking him about his values. He valued time freedom, time in nature, peace and tranquility, financial freedom, accomplishment, and family time. The time freedom, family time, peace and tranquility, and time in nature were lost once he started his own company. He didn't take into consideration the effect this business venture was going to have on his values. Had he brought those values into the decision of starting a company, he could have planned differently to keep his values intact. Maybe he would've

31

negotiated something better with his boss, or maybe started his company with the right people in place to manage the pieces he didn't want, so he could have time freedom, family time, and peace. Using his values to set his goals would've given him the clarity to align his future vision and goals with what's most important to him.

Now that he'd uncovered all his values and taken them into consideration, he could set new goals for his vision. He could bring in a partner to help manage the business so he has more time and freedom. He could bring in an operations manager to handle the company dynamics and human resources. In other words, he had a revised goal list that helped him live a value-aligned life, have family time, and be able to travel again. Make sure that what you want to create aligns with your values.

You've just built the foundation for your best life by understanding your values and allowing them to guide your day-to-day life. You can fuel up and love life by making sure your values show up in your day. You'll make better decisions based on what's truly most important to you. All you create will have meaning because your values are at the base of it. You're on your way to creating meaningful success and a life you love!

I wish, though, it was just values alone that you could stand on. Your new foundation is also going to need the power of self-awareness. To make changes and grow toward that best life that you've always wanted, you need to start seeing yourself and your thoughts. This will allow you to create opportunities and make the best decisions. Every day, you're challenged by all that's going on around you: the environment you're in, the people you're around, and even your own mind. Your awareness is what will keep you on track so you don't fall into old habits and leave your values behind. Your self-awareness will open the door to new choices, allowing you to get out of your own way and finally rise up to the life you know you're capable of living.

The Non-Negotiable You

- Knows their top 5-7 values
- Is intentional about living their values
- Makes decisions based on their values
- Aligns their goals with their values

Action Items

Take Values Assessment

Complete Values in Action

3

YOUR SELF-AWARENESS

Now you have recognized what your values are and how they relate to you, it's time to develop your self-awareness. Self-awareness is the skill of seeing your thoughts, stories and actions clearly. Developing it will allow you to find opportunities for growth. You won't know the changes to make, the actions to take, or the power you hold if you're not self-aware. No more autopilot— I want you to know what you're thinking and choosing. You know the expression "Ignorance is bliss." Change that to "Ignorance is a missed opportunity." If you don't know, you can't grow! One of your most powerful tools is self-awareness, so start using it!

Stephen Covey describes it best in *7 Habits of Highly Effective People* when he explains self-awareness as the ability to stand apart from ourselves and examine our own thinking, attitude, motives, actions, and stories. This is a unique ability that only we as humans possess, yet so few people use it proactively to their advantage. The power of self-awareness is underused because it's misunderstood. People think self-awareness is simply being conscious of what you're doing, but it goes beyond that. Your self-awareness allows you to see what you're experiencing and thinking. It's a separation between you and your thoughts.

Once I illustrate the difference between being conscious and self-aware, you're going to see the importance of creating daily self-awareness. You'll know why it's a habit and daily practice of the non-negotiable you. It's why the first question I ask you in the Morning Mindset is "How do you feel?" Your newfound awareness through your values is what's going to keep you from repeating past behaviors, such as victim mentality, in which we don't accept our own agency. Your awareness is going to lead you to make new and better choices and shift you from self-defeating feelings into empowered thoughts. You can't skip this step; you must have the awareness to create consistent habits and intentions. In the last chapter, we talked about your feelings being created from your environment and circumstances. It's imperative that you bring self-awareness to those feelings in order to respond to them from a value-based place and not become a victim of them.

You are not your feelings.

Think about this simple example: You wake up in the morning irritable. You're a little annoyed, short-tempered, and impatient. You're conscious of how you feel, but that's different from being self-aware. Without self-awareness, you don't interrogate why you feel this way, you just begrudgingly accept your feelings and move through your day irritable and annoyed. You chalk it up to a crap day: "I don't know, I'm just off. It's been like that all day." You can tell how you feel, but you aren't creating the self-awareness that will change it. You're simply feeling as if you have no other choice.

In comparison to being self-aware, if you ask yourself how you feel and answer "off," "a little grumpy," or "annoyed and impatient," you can be proactive in creating positive change versus being defined by your feelings. This step of creating awareness allows you to separate from yourself and examine your thoughts about how you feel, giving you a different perspective and opening the door for you to do something about it. Now you're in a powerful position. I'll be teaching you later in the Morning Mindset how to respond to the feelings that aren't serving you with this new daily awareness.

Consider your self-awareness a gift.

My client Sarah, a business owner, mother, and wife, came to me to level up herself and her team. She wanted to set her sights on bigger and better things and accomplish them.

"I feel like something is missing. I need to accomplish more," she stated, steadfast in her belief.

I could tell she wasn't aware that there was another path to finding a bigger life and that she was just focused on gaining more of what she already had: more success, more mental stimulation, and more accomplishment. Yes, she knew what she valued, but she was hoping to find joy in another finish line, another trophy. She needed to create awareness around how she truly felt and start with herself. She was automatically going toward what usually filled her up without acknowledging how she was feeling. She didn't even know her unhappiness existed.

I let her drive the beginning sessions toward what she thought she wanted. As she reached the accomplishments she was seeking, they fell flat, and they didn't bring her the satisfaction she thought they would.

"Would the lack of spark around your recent successes make you willing to start creating awareness around what you aren't exploring?" I asked her.

She was finally willing to be honest and vulnerable through daily self-awareness, and she found she wasn't truly happy. That awareness, though painful, opened the door for her to do something about her situation. Rather than continuing to search for the next good thing and continually missing the mark, she explored her values through a different lens.

People avoid self-awareness when they associate shame or guilt with the discovery. If you treat it that way, you'll avoid self-awareness as an act of self-preservation. Your discoveries aren't meant to be judged or make you feel bad about yourself, this self-awareness is a gift. When you learn about an area where you have an opportunity to better your life, that's something to be excited about and grateful for, not ashamed of. When you reframe your thoughts around self-awareness, you'll be more willing to see what you need to.

The awareness of how you feel is like a confession of honesty, and that alone can cause a dramatic shift in the way you understand yourself. As I mentioned in the first chapter, it's hard for people to be honest with themselves—they don't want to say what they don't want to know. But guess what? You already know it, you just aren't saying it—which is only feeding the underlying issue. I see it all the time. You think that if you don't say what's bothering you, then it's not real and you don't have to deal with it. You're right about not having to deal with what's bothering you, but subconsciously it's still affecting you. If you don't create awareness around your situation, you give up your power to change it.

My client Ben experienced this. He was feeling off for a few days and couldn't articulate why.

"I just feel off, like something isn't right, and it's getting in the way of my work and relationships. It's affecting my attitude," he said.

"Okay, define feeling 'off,' what does that mean?" I asked.

"I don't know, I can't quite explain it. It's hard to put my finger on it."

I could tell there was something he didn't want to say. "Feeling off" was a safe way of explaining what was going on, but it was keeping him from knowing how to do anything about it. If he didn't have awareness of how he was really feeling, how could he ever change it?

"What don't you want to say about how you're feeling?" I asked him.

"Oh!" he replied. "That's a good question. I guess I just feel like I'm under a lot of pressure. I feel like everyone around me depends on me to have the answers and to make things happen, and sometimes I don't know if I can pull it all off. It's stressful," he said freely. I could hear the relief from his confession.

"What's hard about saying that?" I asked.

"I guess I just think I shouldn't have any negative thoughts, that if I think that way, it's not going to do me any good." Now he was being honest with himself and could have movement in the ultimate outcome of the situation.

While he may not have been saying his negative thoughts aloud, he was certainly thinking them subconsciously. The lack of admitting it wasn't keeping it from being true, his omission only blocked the truth from being worked through, leaving him confused and stuck. With Ben's newfound self-awareness, he could now take action to change those deeper feelings and get back on track.

Awareness of your thoughts is the
foundation to mastering your mindset.

When you aren't creating daily awareness, you miss out on opportunities. You stay defined by how you feel and accept it instead of challenging it. The other day, my client Jennifer said, "I had the best thing happen the other day with my awareness in the Morning Mindset journal."

I could tell how excited she was to share.

"I was thinking about how I felt, and all of a sudden, I found myself writing about this deal that I'm working on that feels really difficult to make happen. I realized that I felt like not even trying anymore because it felt too hard and like a waste of time. Once I wrote that, I instantly perked up and thought, 'Oh no, I will not quit on this.' I became so motivated to take serious action and was fired up. I would've never known what was blocking my success if I hadn't asked myself how I was feeling. I would've missed this opportunity!"

What are you ignoring that could be blocking great opportunities? That's where you could be turning a blind eye. Sometimes we steer awareness away from issues and feelings because we don't want to deal with them but that avoidance creates missed opportunities. Once you understand that you are not your feelings, your self awareness becomes a tool of empowerment. Take a minute right now and check in with yourself; is there anything you aren't facing? Do you avoid looking at the details of your finances? Do you ignore that you're not aligned with your business partners? Do you rarely take a vacation or time for yourself? Do you know you need to devote more attention to a relationship?

What if you did create awareness around the areas of your life that might feel a bit intimidating or uncomfortable? The fear is that you'll make it worse, but the reality is that you have a chance to make it better. The non-negotiable you faces those areas of awareness and welcomes the opportunity to improve them. For some, gathering awareness is enough of a start. You don't have an immediate obligation to do something with it. In fact, sitting with your awareness in the present can offer perspective before you make decisions. For others, since you're growing and becoming empowered, you'll be motivated by your new insights. For now, take away the pressure of having to immediately do something about what you uncover about yourself. We have time to work with the issues through the consistency of the Morning Mindset. I'll be teaching you how to make conscious choices so you'll be able to choose what to do with that awareness. There will be times you'll create awareness but decide to not take action. That's okay, it's your choice, and you're going to have the trust in yourself to make that choice. Let's make creating awareness the only action you're responsible for right now.

Your new awareness will be a shining light for you to see more than you have before. When you get into the habit of being self-aware, you turn on the light to see the path in front of you. You'll have more choices and be empowered to grow for the better. Living in awareness requires you to commit to seeing yourself, your thoughts, and your surroundings consistently. Awareness of your thoughts is the foundation to mastering your mindset. I've said this before, and I will say it many times in this book: It's imperative that you have control over your mind. You can't choose your thoughts if you aren't consciously aware in the moment. We'll expand on this in the next chapter with a deeper dive into becoming present, which is the time when you can create all you want and need.

"I'm painfully aware now" is what my clients say to me after they start living in a state of awareness and experiencing honesty with themselves. That's music to my ears, because I know the process is working and they're starting to see their thoughts. Growth requires a degree of pain; it's uncomfortable, but if they didn't have that awareness, there wouldn't be any opportunity to lean into challenges to change and grow. No one wants to actively be in pain, but trust me, the uncomfortable feeling is short-lived. You'll go through a few days of saying you can't believe how often you say this or do that—mirrors of ourselves can be hard to face—but then you'll start to take action that creates change. You'll make a better decision that aligns with your values. When you're aware, you'll want to make the best decision. You'll want to take action that's going to create joy and avoid stress.

Oftentimes people come to me wanting change but lack the clarity about where. Self-awareness holds the clarity you are looking for! Reviewing core life pillars is an excellent place to start and will reveal where you want change or growth. Core life pillars include. relationships, career, finances, mental health, and physical health. If you were to assess each one of those on a scale of 1-10, with one being the least satisfied and ten being the most satisfied, how would you rate them? Now think about what rating you would like those areas of your life to have. That gap between your current ratings and your desired ratings is the awareness that begins the change. Be careful not to define high ratings against societal norms; you get to define your own ten. What the best career looks like to one person will be different for another, so don't compare. Make note of these areas of awareness as we continue to move through the foundational work and the Morning Mindset. To fully understand the control you can have over your mind, we need to talk about consciousness. When I refer to being conscious, I don't mean being awake or alert. I'm referring to a deeper level of awareness, one where you're seeing and hearing your own thoughts and can be discerning about them. In the simplest scenario, consider when you hit the snooze button on your alarm and regret it later. You likely weren't making a conscious choice, weighing the pros and cons of your decision and understanding what's motivating your choice. On the contrary you were acting unconsciously, in auto pilot mode based on your usual habits. You make decisions in this manner all day long—you eat something unhealthy, you skip the gym, you have an extra drink, you say something you wish you hadn't, you procrastinate on a project, you avoid a difficult conversation, you waste time on social media—usually all unconsciously. Yes, you know what you're doing, but do you know why you're doing it? You aren't consciously choosing that option in the moment. Take a minute to reflect on the last 24 hours. Can you recall five decisions you made that have you wondering why or how you did them? Write them down and create awareness right now. For example:

- I agreed to go to an event I didn't want to attend.
- I stopped working on an important project and gave my time away.
- I overbooked myself and had to cancel a personal appointment.
- I put off a decision again for the third day in a row.

- I got sucked into social media for thirty minutes.

Awareness will provide the opportunity to look at your decisions and make more conscious choices around the way you're living your life. It's a tool that the non-negotiable you will use to constantly guide yourself in the right direction.

If you're determined to be the person who's capable of creating the success and joy they want, then you have to stop making the path overly complicated. You now have your values and understand how to reframe your feelings through self-awareness. The road to success can be simple if you're committed to the next step: controlling your mind so it works for you, not against you.

The Non-Negotiable You

- Is self-aware
- Knows they are not their feelings
- Views awareness as an opportunity
- Uses self-awareness to make conscious choices

Action Items

Take the Life Assessment

4

YOUR MINDSET MATTERS

Your mind holds a great deal of power and produces thoughts to protect you from failure, embarrassment, and judgment. Your mind wants to keep you safe and comfortable, but it can also hold you back from creating and living your best life. When you're in control of the power your mind holds, you can use it to your advantage. Otherwise, you'll fall victim to the thoughts your mind feeds you. Knowing your values and having your new skill of self-awareness is an advantage when learning to control your mind. You want your mind to be your partner, not an obstacle, in creating meaningful success and a life you love. The non-negotiable you is in control of their mind.

I bet you've said at some point, "I know I'm capable of more." You're right, but you won't figure out what you're capable of until you start controlling your mind. It's your responsibility to filter your thoughts, to keep the ones you want, and ditch the ones that don't serve you. Second to being happy, the most requested change people want from coaching is a shift in mindset. Clients tell me all the time, "I want to change my mindset. I want to be more positive. I want to live in peace. I want to be fearless. I want to have an abundance mindset. How do I even start?"

Right Here, Right Now

Before I take you down the path of changing your mindset, you need to understand that controlling your mind happens in the present moment. The most common mindset issues people encounter are living in the past or projecting into the future. The past is over, and the future is not here yet. Therefore, the foundation of changing your mindset for positive growth has to be you living in the present moment.

The past carries everything that's already happened, and you can't change it. When your mind goes back to replay negative events, it creates regret, remorse, and guilt. The repeated thoughts of regret and remorse will affect your confidence, which affects your mindset! If you're living in the future, you're likely creating worry, anxiety, and stress over something that hasn't, and may never, happen. Your mind becomes stuck trying to figure out the outcome of a situation that you can't predict or control. The fix comes from using your awareness to catch those moments when your thoughts are drifting into the past or future and correct yourself. These four simple words, *right here right now,* bring your attention back to the present moment where you have the power to control your mind.

Here are the most common mindset struggles:

- A scarcity mindset—you worry there isn't enough of something (time, money, business, love)
- A low-confidence mindset—you don't see your true value and capabilities
- A negative mindset—you see things through a negative lens
- A limited mindset—you don't think you're capable of more
- A fixed mindset —you only see things one way and lack open mindedness

All of these mindsets are based on experiences and beliefs from the past, or fears and worries for the future—definitely not the present moment. Letting your self-awareness alert you to when you're worried about the future or stuck in the past will set you up for success in changing your mindset in the present.

Building your ideal mindset starts with the thoughts you give your mind to work with. If you want a more positive mindset, you're going to have to choose positive thoughts. If you think negative, doubting thoughts, your mindset will be negative. If you want a less limited mindset, you need to think more thoughts about your capabilities. Should scarcity be your mindset, then practicing counter-thoughts of abundance will help you shift your mindset. The decisions you make about your mindset set you up to create meaningful success and a life you love, so they shouldn't be overlooked.

You now have your values to lead you in the right direction, and your daily awareness to help you see opportunities for change. Next, you need to ensure that your thoughts are also in alignment. Unfortunately, they don't always match up. You can know your values and how to live them through goals and decisions, but if you aren't in control of your mind, you'll constantly be challenged by the thoughts that creep in unintentionally. You can create awareness, but if you aren't controlling your thoughts, you won't take the action to make the change. It's those unwanted thoughts you didn't create that can have you falling back into old habits, straying away from your values and what you truly want.

Your mind has operated by calling the shots for a long time, but not in a way that empowers you. If you reflect on your daily decisions, you'll find that most of them are made based on your mind's response to everything around you. Your mind is continuously feeding off your environment, your circumstances, your feelings, other people's opinions, past experiences, and anything else it chooses to grab onto. It's your job to give it something different to respond to.

You have to feed your mind what you want it to consume.

It's helpful to understand how your mind feeds off your environment from a positive standpoint first. If you're at a sporting event and the crowd is going wild, you feel the energy and change with it. In a sales environment, you likely excel when the team is all in one place, feeding off the energy and competition from other people. Those moments of contagious energy are an example of your mind feeding off the environment. Have you ever worked out at home versus in a group class setting? For most people, it's night and day from a performance perspective. This is why they say to surround yourself with great people and stay away from energy vampires. Your mind feeds off the environment and circumstances around you. The reality is that life doesn't always set us up to be in the environments that serve us best. You might be working your dream job but have a Negative Nancy in your office. You can't control her, but you can control the way you receive her and respond to her. You don't have to be a victim to her energy. We can't always rely on being in the best of circumstances or around the most inspiring people, so you have to play the leading role in controlling your mind. Sometimes your mind feeds off great energies and it works in your favor by providing you with good guidance, but oftentimes it's not the best guide without your conscious influence. You have to feed your mind what you want it to consume.

If you think back to a time when you were pulled in by your environment, good or bad, you'll remember how susceptible you were to what was going on around you. As I stressed in Chapter Three, it's imperative that you're highly aware of what's going on inside you in the moment. You now have the foundation of creating self-awareness, but we're going to up the ante by taking that concept into your everyday decisions. You have to be ready to consciously assess how your thoughts and actions will align with your values. Only then can you choose the thought that will empower you to make a decision that will ultimately get you closer to your best life.

What's challenging about being in a conscious state of awareness and controlling your mindset is that we live in a society full of distractions, demands, and ideals. You're repeatedly pulled in several directions, which entices you to multitask. You don't feel you have the time to even consider making a conscious decision or getting control of your thoughts. Social media and smartphones bombard you with constant interruptions and distractions, with the flow of people's opinions always trying to invade your mind and influence your actions. At any given moment, you can be thrown off a course of action that appeared to be right just hours before. Being conscious was much easier 35 years ago when we didn't have the distractions we have today. Awareness and commitment to understanding your thoughts in the present can combat those distractions.

My client Kelly, a real estate brokerage owner, was troubled about how she wasn't taking advantage of the opportunities she had to lead her management team. Empowering her team and growing her brand aligned with her values, so she couldn't understand why she wasn't taking action toward that value.

"It's frustrating, I look back later in the day and think, 'Why did I do that?' I gave the answer instead of asking the question. I acted as a manager instead of empowering them as a leader. I know what I should be doing, but I'm not doing it."

I could see her searching within herself for the answer. I knew she needed to explore where she was in the moments when she was called to lead.

"When you gave the answer instead of asking the question, what thoughts were going through your mind?"

"I was thinking about the next action I needed to take. I have so much to do and never enough time."

This instantly gave me insight into her scarcity mindset around time. She also realized for herself that she wasn't present in the moment to make the decision that aligned with her values; she was distracted by other tasks she had to do. The recurring thought that there wasn't enough time created the feeling that she needed to move fast, always be one step ahead, but it was costing her. She was missing out on opportunities to lead.

"What needs to change?" I asked.

"I need to slow down and be conscious of the moment I'm in so I can make the choice that aligns with my values."

She was able to see how her mindset could lead her in the wrong direction if she wasn't aware of her thoughts and how they affected her choices.

Once you start every day being aware, you'll find opportunities all day long to examine your thoughts and feelings, empowering you to make better choices. To control your mind, it's helpful to understand the cycle of thoughts, feelings, and actions that your mind uses to springboard from one element to the next. It's a cycle that you need to have a say in or you'll be on the road to Victimville. A thought in your mind creates a feeling in you, and that feeling inspires action. Take these thought-feeling-action examples:

You're a few weeks out from your first marathon and doubt creeps in.

- Thought: I'm never going to be able to finish the race.
- Feeling: The fear of failure.
- Action: That feeling causes you to not compete, thus deviating from the intention you committed to.

You're trying to lose weight and the scale hasn't changed.

- Thought: None of this works, what does it matter anyway?
- Feeling: Hopelessness and disappointment.

- Action: Those feelings cause you to skip the gym or go back to eating unhealthily again.

If you continue to repeat cycles like this, you'll lose confidence in your abilities and lack trust in yourself. You'll be in a negative mindset, but you won't see it as that simple to change because you confused yourself with all the feelings. Those feelings compound over time and hold you back from being great! It doesn't have to be that way.

I want you to start considering your thoughts as optional.

Your mind is going to present a thought to you, it's up to you to be aware and consciously choose whether to accept it or not. When your mind offers up a thought you don't like, say, "No, thank you." In the examples above, instead of saying, "I'm going to fail," simply say, "No, thanks," and choose a different thought. One that's aligned with your values will create a different feeling. There are endless thoughts to choose from instead:

- "I'll feel great even if I only try."
- "I'm going to win."
- "I'll do my best."
- "I've got this."
- "I'll never know unless I try."
- "It will be fun either way."

Your new thought will change your feeling from fear to excitement or willingness, which in turn inspires the action to go for it. I use this process all the time. Today I was aware that I didn't feel like writing. My mind was telling me that it was too challenging today, but my values and integrity told me that I needed to take action toward what's most important to me, what I committed to. So I changed my thoughts and chose to think:

- "I'm a great writer."
- "I love seeing the words come together and reading the complete thoughts."

- "I love the feeling of accomplishment when I'm done."
- "I'm passionate about making an impact."
- "I'm committed to authoring this book."

Just like that, my new thoughts created a new feeling, and I was ready to take action and write my next chapter.

Choosing your thoughts is your most underused superpower! As the gatekeeper of your mind, your best interests must be the priority. I want you to start thinking of your thoughts as optional:

- Does this thought I'm being offered help me or hurt me?
- Do I want to keep it or choose something different?

You have that superpower, you just haven't been using it. You haven't been aware enough to see that you have that choice. Your mind is not the boss of you, even though many people act as though it is. They feel, "If I think it, then it must be the case." Not the case. You can choose differently. You don't have to accept all of your mind's ideas, especially if they're not based on a conscious, self-aware thinking process. It's your responsibility to acknowledge the thought you're being offered and then decide if you want it or not.

You can't make the best decisions from an unconscious state.

I have people ask me all the time, "Why do I always make decisions that aren't good for me?" The answer is, you're making decisions from an unaware place based on what your mind feeds you instead of your values. Most people don't intentionally make poor choices, so it feels like it happened *to* you, which creates a victim mentality. We will discuss feeling like a victim as a block to your best life in the next chapter.

When we make poor decisions because of a critical or fearful mind, we have to contend with regret. Nothing takes us more out of the present than regret. We spend all our time wondering, "Why did I do that? Why did I say yes to that? What would make me say that?" Those are likely questions you ask when you make unconscious decisions. It's like you weren't even there to make the decision! Here is a simple example: You might be out with friends, having a great time, and drinks are flowing.

"Can I get you another drink?" you hear the bartender ask.

"Sure," you respond.

No thought involved, just a reactive answer. You just made an unconscious decision. That decision was based on what your mind was feeding off: the energy in the room, the feel-good sensation, maybe friends saying to have another one. You can't make the best decisions from an unconscious state.

Fast-forward to the next day, and you can't get up. You're tired and unmotivated, and instead of jumping up and taking on the day, you regret staying out.

In contrast, a conscious decision would look like asking yourself:

- Do I want another drink?
- How many have I had?
- How will this affect my evening, and how will it affect my day tomorrow?
- Am I okay with the possible outcome if I say yes?

You thought about the options, the effects, the rewards, and the consequences. You made a decision from a place of awareness, considering the effect your decision could have on the life you enjoy and love. You used your mind to make a conscious decision that started with you. I'm not trying to get you to say no to the drink, I just want you to have a say in the decisions you make that affect your life. If socializing with friends to burn off steam from a long day is part of a value, then stay! I want you to be empowered in that driver's seat! There's a huge difference when you can reflect on a decision and know that you made it consciously versus regretting it and thinking, "Why did I let that happen?"

When you make conscious decisions, you also take responsibility. If you made a conscious decision to stay out longer, there isn't regret the next morning. You thought about it in the moment, weighed it against your values, made a conscious decision, and you moved on. You may not physically feel great if you overindulged, but you won't have the emotional pain and regret to deal with. Your responsibility accepts the consequences if there are any. On the flip side, if you made an unconscious decision, you probably have a knot in the pit of your stomach created by regret. You're thinking, "Why did I do that?" That regret might turn into shame and cause you to start questioning yourself: "Why do I make the decisions I make?" This is because you don't trust yourself, which we will cover more in-depth in Chapter Seven. There's a snowball effect when you aren't aware of the decisions you're making.

Saying yes to one thing is saying no to something else.

My client Evan, a certified financial planner, was avoiding business development, a key part of his business's growth and asset accumulation. The first week, he seemed to be content with his reasons for lack of action. But by week two, regret was showing up. He was disappointed about not taking action toward something that aligned with his values.

"I have this huge goal, and I know I can do it, but it's never going to happen if I don't create the connections and opportunities needed to get me there. I keep doing other activities instead of the one I need to focus on most," he shared with me.

His confession clued me in that he wasn't happy with the choice he was making. I'd also worked with him for over a year, so I knew he was a producer and achiever. He wasn't making this decision intentionally.

"Tell me about the activities you're doing instead."

"So many different distractions. A friend needs help with their business. A client wants to grab lunch. Someone wants to pop by the office to say hi. Don't get me wrong, these are all important to me. I want to help my friends and be available to people."

"Okay. What's motivating you to say yes."

"I want to be a good person. I like to help."

"Is there any reason you would say no?"

"No. Wait, yes."

In that moment, I knew he wasn't making a conscious decision, weighing the effects or consequences of his choices. He was making them based on his feelings in the moment and not looking at what he was saying no to: his goals, intentions, and values.

"What are you learning?"

"I didn't realize that when I said yes to these other things that I wanted to do, I was really saying no to what I was trying to achieve."

Now that you understand what a conscious decision looks like and how you can have control of your mind, you have the platform to make decisions that align with your values. You have to make conscious decisions to choose what's most important to you. That will keep you on track toward your best life. Think about that alarm going off in the morning for you to get up and exercise. If your values are physical activity and feeling capable and competent, you'll need to be self-aware to make a decision based on your values. Your mind is going to form a thought based on what's going on in the moment — your environment, circumstances, and feelings. The alarm will go off, and your mind will probably tell you that the bed is so warm, it's so dark out, and that you don't really need to work out this morning. With those thoughts, you'll snuggle in and hit the snooze button. Thoughts, feelings, action. In that moment, you're being controlled by your mind instead of you controlling your mind. This is where your awareness and values step in and feed your mind what it needs to hear to lead you to your best life. You say "No, thank you," to the thoughts your mind is feeding you about a warm, cozy bed, and instead say, "I will feel capable and competent when I get up and get my physical activity in." Once you start controlling your mind, you know better. You become aware of these thoughts and you take over and choose differently. It's your responsibility to be aware of this choice and remind yourself that your values are being physically healthy and feeling capable and competent. You've already learned that when your values show up, you're more fulfilled and have more energy. That understanding you have of your values will lead you to make a value-based decision and live a value-aligned life. If you fall victim to what your mind feeds you about your warm bed and flexible schedule, you don't stand a chance, and you'll be having a date with regret later in the day.

Sometimes our conscious decisions, such as to grow a business or achieve a key goal, can go sideways, and we think we're controlling our minds when we've really lost perspective. For example, at one point in my coaching practice I was working nonstop.

"Why are you working twelve hours a day?" my husband asked me.

He knew this wasn't in alignment with my values and what I wanted. His words were a surprise to me, almost as if I didn't even know I'd been working that much, not consciously aware. I had gotten wrapped up in helping as many people as I could. I loved coaching and supporting people in changing their lives, but it was costing me my values: my family time, physical health, personal growth, and time freedom. I had to get back to making choices about my life with a conscious mind.

Responding versus reacting is a key element of controlling your mind.

The ability to choose your thoughts leads to choosing your responses. Oftentimes the regret you experience from past events comes from reacting to situations without first taking the time to get control of your mind and emotions. There probably isn't a day that goes by where you don't feel some bit of frustration from a situation. How you handle that emotion depends on your ability to control your mind. For instance, say someone cuts you off on the road and you react by speeding around them to cut them off or giving them a not-so-friendly hand gesture. Your heart is racing—that's a reaction. You had no control there, and you took action with little or no thought at all. In contrast, when you get cut off, you could feel the emotion come up, pause to take control of your mind, remove the emotion, and decide what you want to do. That's a controlled response from a place of awareness. When you insert that pause, you're becoming intentional about how you want to deal with the situation. That's having control of your mind!

Responding versus reacting is a key element of controlling your mind. In intense emotional situations, it's not uncommon for your mind to tell you that you're being attacked, which can produce the reaction to fight back, get defensive, or protect yourself. The self-aware person in control of their mind pauses, evaluates the story that the mind is creating, and then decides what to do with it. Your conscious mind is discerning and in control so you can choose the right path, avoiding regret later. Repeated regret is a confidence killer and doubt creator. Once you start responding with intention, you build confidence in your actions and trust that you can lead yourself correctly.

Take a minute to reflect on your reactions over the last few days. Can you recall and write down three to five moments when you reacted? What self-awareness can you create around the cause of the reaction? How could you have responded instead?

Mary, a client of mine who owns a recruiting firm, was becoming exhausted from the repeated emotional reactions that were taking place with clients. The relationship between the company looking to hire and the recruiter in search of the candidates can be a highly charged relationship. Expectations and emotions are high, and it can make for a very reactive environment.

"I'm just tired of being beat up. These clients are stressed, and they want the end result now. They bring all their stress and emotion to the conversation, and then I have to defend everything we're doing and calm them down. I just want peace."

As soon as she said "defend," I could hear the personal emotion that was causing a reaction instead of a response.

"I can hear you feeling like you're being beat up and attacked. If we took that out of the equation and you weren't emotionally charged, how would you respond then?" I asked.

She had to think about it for a few minutes, and I could see her posture changing, literally relaxing. "I would ask them questions about why they're frustrated or what it would look like if things were further along."

There was peace in her answer, and that would bring peace to her conversations. She was now in a place of controlling her mind and responding instead of reacting. She was choosing thoughts and actions that aligned with the peaceful mindset she now understood she wanted.

What mindset do you want? An abundance mindset? A limitless mindset? A positive mindset? You affirm the state of mind you want to be in by choosing thoughts and actions that align with that mindset. If you want an abundant, limitless, positive mindset, you get rid of thoughts like "I don't have enough" and you choose thoughts like "I have plenty," "I can make more," and "I have all that I need." You change your actions to stop hoarding and start giving. You stop racing and slow down. Don't overcomplicate it. This isn't rocket science. It's you being aware of what you want and controlling your mind to think and act in accordance with it.

Mastering your mindset is one of the greatest victories you'll have in our time together. It's going to take daily, intentional action, which is why it's a step in the Morning Mindset. The control you have over your mind and thoughts will set you up to live in alignment with your values and take action toward what you want in your life. As you embrace this new, empowered you, it's going to be essential that you take responsibility for creating that meaningful success and a life you love. No one else is going to do it for you!

The Non-Negotiable You

- Lives in the present moment
- Chooses their thoughts
- Responds instead of reacts

5

YOUR RESPONSIBILITY

Your new understanding of how to control your mindset brings opportunities to set intentions around what you want in your life. You've identified your values, you're self-aware, and you're able to control your thoughts. The next step is to make sure you understand your responsibility not to become a victim and get derailed from creating what you want. Before you practice conscious awareness of your values and understand the control you can have over your mind, you're in a default life. In the default life, it's convenient and easy to fall victim to what's happened to you because your choices lack conscious intention. It's hard to see where you have control and where you can make different choices. That old way of thinking is changing here and now. The non-negotiable you takes responsibility for creating the life and success you want!

Becoming focused on creating your best life doesn't come magically, it takes a daily practice of setting intentions with the goal of meeting your values and creating what you want in your life. You have a say in your day and need to take responsibility for that. When you don't take responsibility, that's when the victim mentality slips into your mindset.

You might be thinking, "Victim mentality, that's not an issue for me." Hear me out. Whether you recognize it or not, everyone falls into moments of victim mentality. Even my most successful clients fall into the trap at times. It shows up in the most unsuspecting ways, like lack of sleep, running out of time, family obligations, and over-committing; but with daily awareness, they can catch it and choose differently. I remember being a kid, crying to my stepdad any time someone hurt my feelings or upset me. Back then it was little things, but they seemed huge at the time, like friends being mean or boyfriends breaking my heart. He would say, "Only what you allow Angela, only what you allow." It made no sense to me as a kid, but as I got older and learned what "mindset" was, it became crystal clear. It was up to me how I would allow situations to affect me. I had a choice. I didn't have to be a victim of someone else's words or actions. No one else is responsible for my feelings and actions, only I am. Embracing this simple truth shifts you from being a victim to being empowered.

**In your best life, you make conscious
choices and take ownership of them.**

Even my very successful, happy clients experience a victim mentality amidst their joy. It's not easy constantly taking responsibility for the choices we make, it takes awareness and honesty. It's adulting in a big way, when sometimes it's enticing to just rest on your laurels and accept what life is throwing at you. Do you remember the last time you slept in because you "couldn't" get up? Victim. How about the exercise class you missed because you "didn't have time"? Victim. These are minor examples, but it's the habit and language that are making you the victim in these situations. You're creating a subconscious habit of being a victim and getting further away from your best life. Let's look at these examples:

"I chose to get more sleep to recharge and feel rested." This is taking responsibility for a choice you're making to feel rested and healthy. You made a conscious choice to have more rest.

"I overslept. I couldn't get up this morning because I was so tired." This is being a victim. Your mind is saying you didn't have a choice in the matter.

"I chose to miss my exercise class and decided to spend the time with my family." That's responsibility. You made a conscious choice to choose your family over your exercise.

"I couldn't get to my exercise class because I had to get home to my family." This is a victim statement saying you had to, that you didn't have a choice.

As a victim, you give your power away, but in your best life, you make conscious choices and take ownership of them.

Responsibility directs your mind
toward creating solutions.

Once you allow yourself to be a victim, you take away your ability to change and figure out a solution to avoid it happening again. You'll repeat the same pattern again and again because you allowed it to happen before. Fast-forward weeks later, and you still haven't made it to your exercise class because you still "don't have time," and you feel awful. You question why you can't stay committed and wonder when you'll ever have time. You feel burnt out because your values aren't being met. You go through this vicious cycle of guilt, blame, and self-pity. In contrast, if you just took ownership of your decision, you would open up the space to figure out how to change your circumstances. You might say, "I'm not going to exercise class because I choose not to prioritize it, but I will on Wednesday. Today I choose to spend time with my family." You're taking responsibility to receive what you want.

When you take responsibility, you create awareness and start to see your options; you become empowered. When you're aware of your decision, you'll usually choose what aligns with your values. Most people don't want to sabotage themselves intentionally. If you still decide to go in the opposite direction of what's best for you, you can have the awareness that you did it and make better choices down the road. Responsibility directs your mind toward creating solutions. This empowers your mind to look for a solution, either in the present or the future. Victimization tells the mind that you don't have a choice and that there's nothing you can do.

In one of my group sessions, a client named Joanne, who's an overachiever both professionally and personally, was repeating a story for a few weeks. She was exceeding her goals at work, but she was feeling off because she hadn't had the time to get her morning routine in and her workouts weren't consistent. She'd had some recent changes: a new dog, a promotion, and new challenges at work. I knew she had the ability to create self-awareness because she was committed to her Morning Mindset, so I was able to give her space before I stepped in.

"I just don't have time. I can't get my schedule in order. It's hard. I have a new dog, and he throws the schedule off. And with the growth in my business, I have more clients that need me," she said.

I could see the look in her eyes that she'd figured it out for herself.

"I'm a victim...I've never thought of myself as having a victim mentality, but it's happening," she said. "This is ridiculous. People get dogs all the time, their business grows, nothing is happening to me that I can't handle and figure out. Tomorrow, I'm back to planning my day in the morning and getting back to the gym!"

Her daily practice of awareness, which we had coached her on, allowed her to see for herself what was happening and take responsibility to change. So yes, even highly successful people fall into the trap of being a victim.

Excuses and distractions make being a victim convenient, but intentions and values will deflect that behavior.

It's not natural to take responsibility for our actions, or lack thereof. Remember, you learned in the last chapter that your mind is always feeding off your environment, circumstances, feelings, and other people's thoughts. That's why we worked on mindset first. If you can control those thoughts, you're less likely to have life happen "to" you, causing you to be a victim. You always have a choice, it's a matter of whether or not you're aware of it and taking responsibility to make that choice.

Excuses and distractions make being a victim convenient, but intentions and values will trip the switch every time. In the Morning Mindset, we work on intentions from a place of awareness that starts with you for this very reason. I can't tell you how many times I've tricked myself into believing something was important enough to be worth skipping out on a commitment I made to myself. In the past, I've scheduled time to write a blog post but started on a client proposal knowing I wouldn't have enough time to do both because my mind told me that the client is more important. I was aware enough to know the truth that the client proposal was just a handy excuse. The reality was that I would've rather worked on that proposal than write a blog post. It would've been easy to fall into a victim mentality if I hadn't known my values, but I did. So I went back to them, made my conscious decision, and moved forward.

Emails, texts, and social media seem to be the biggest culprits when it comes to distractions. At least once a day I hear "I got stuck in my emails," or "I got sucked into social media," or "I just keep getting interrupted with texts." Those are all victim statements. You let yourself get stuck, sucked in, and distracted. Being consciously aware of your choices will help you avoid being a victim.

Often the consequence of what you think you have to do is grossly overexaggerated in your head, causing you to fall victim to your own thoughts.

This was the case for a client named Jeremy, who had just launched his private financial advisory firm and was exhausted. Building a business takes valuable energy resources.

"I'm up so late working. I have research to do, I have writing that needs to get done for marketing. I have to get some traction with the business and become profitable," he says.

"What happens if you don't stay up writing and researching every night?" I questioned.

He sat there a minute and then shrugged his shoulders sheepishly, "Nothing I guess. I'd work on it the next day."

"Yes, that's the reality of it," I said. "But what I really want to know is, what were the thoughts driving your actions?"

"Fear, I guess. I don't want the business to fail. My family has sacrificed a lot for me to take this leap. I don't want to disappoint them," were his words.

"Is that going to happen? Given your record of success, your drive, and your determination, will it happen?"

"No."

The truth is, when you're living in that victim mentality and redlining your physical and mental capacity, you don't have the bandwidth to create something amazing. You're giving from an empty tank and a disempowered position if you aren't aware and in control of your thoughts. Your best chance of creating a strong, thriving business is by living your values, taking care of your needs, and making empowered, intentional choices. You can fall victim to what your mind feeds you or choose a different thought that will empower you to make a great choice. The mind is a powerful thing, and I promise you, you want to be controlling it and using it to your advantage, not the other way around.

Your awareness and honesty will keep you from falling into that victim mentality and placing the blame elsewhere. The consequences won't be the failure or negativity your mind is trying to sell you. It's simply a matter of awareness that's going to keep you from being a victim!

You don't have to be a victim to all the spinning plates in your life and the juggling you're doing on a daily basis. Take a look at any intense work commitments, family obligations, and whatever else is holding you back from your values, and ask yourself these important questions:

- Does this need my attention now?
- Could I delegate this?
- Could I schedule this for a later time?
- Does this align with my values?
- What has me saying yes?

In asking these questions, you can create awareness around the demand and a new reality for yourself. If you don't ask these questions, you won't be conscious that you're pulling away from your values. You'll be creating the perfect environment for running on empty and living on excuses in a victim mentality, like:

- "I couldn't get there on time because I have too many commitments scheduled."
- "I had to answer a client's call, so I missed the soccer game."
- "I need to finish these emails, so I'll be home late."
- "I had to volunteer for an event."

You may think all the reasons behind your actions are true, but if you look closer at your intentions, I'll bet they're not. Either way, empower yourself to go back to your values, be conscious in the decision, and start taking responsibility for those choices. They didn't just happen to you. Then you can stand behind your decisions, take responsibility, and do away with the choices made for you as a victim of circumstance.

I'm not here to judge you. You have to know what feeds you. Take responsibility for making conscious choices and steer clear of victimization. When you start changing your language to take responsibility for the choices you make, you aren't a victim anymore.

I was meeting with a client named Fran the other day, and she sat down and smiled wide.

"How are you?" I asked.

"Good! Really, really good!" she replied, still smiling like there was something she was dying to tell me.

"Yeah? What's so good right now?"

"I'm so aware! I've been so honest with myself about everything. I'm so present, I can feel every word I write in my Morning Mindset journal. I'm trusting myself when I create my intentions and the responsibility feels *so* good!"

This is the progression of your state of being when doing the Morning Mindset. It's so simple that you can almost doubt it, but consistent confidence in your conscious choices at the start of the day will keep you rigorously aligned, more so than any other practice I've seen.

When you're a victim, you lack the power to take authority over a situation.

In one group session, I was talking about being a victim and making choices consciously. One of the members is a business owner, husband, and father, and the three roles constantly compete for his time. Most of his choices were being made from a victim mentality—he didn't have time to do the work, or he didn't get to spend time with his son because of work. He had the best of intentions, but he wasn't conscious in his choices and taking responsibility for them. He called me two days later.

"I want to take my son to the beach, but I feel guilty with all the work I should be doing."

"What would your choice be if you aligned with your values?" I asked him. I knew he could be honest and aware of himself if he got out of his victim mentality.

"What I need to do for work could be done tomorrow, and I need some time with my son."

He got off the phone confident that he was making a conscious decision. He was excited to report back later that he had no guilt at the beach, he did what he needed to do the next day, and he felt amazing!

When you're a victim, you lack the power to take authority over a situation. Over the years, I've worked with hundreds of real estate agents who easily fell into a victim mentality when the inventory was low, and it's not uncommon for the market to go through inventory cycles. They say, "Nothing is available, so I can't sell." It's that victim mentality that wants to pull them to the sideline until the market allows them to come back. In other words, they say the market has control over their business. Yes, the circumstances create a challenge, but challenges can be overcome as long as you aren't a victim and you find gratitude for the challenge, which I'll explain in the Morning Mindset practice. My most successful agents love a difficult market because they take responsibility for it and figure out what they can do, which gives them the upper hand against the competition.

Once you shift from a victim mentality to taking responsibility, you start to ask, "What can I do?" You come up with actions that can be set as intentions for your day, ensuring that you're taking responsibility for what you want. The real estate agents saw that they could create inventory instead of waiting for it to appear. When faced with a challenge, an empowered mindset starts to look for solutions instead of just focusing on the problem and waiting for it to change.

If you think about your day, I bet you can find a moment where you shifted the blame and said you couldn't do something because of someone or something else. Take a minute and make a list of situations where you might be showing up as the victim. Think about what it would look like for you to take responsibility and set an intention around it. Instead of thinking, "Work and family keep me too busy, so I never have time for myself," set an intention to carve out fifteen minutes for yourself. Or instead of saying, "I never get to unplug because my clients need to be able to reach me," set an intention to let your clients know you'll be unavailable for a short period of time but will get back to them afterward. Shining a light on those occurrences provides you with a valuable opportunity to take responsibility and set an intention, putting you back in control.

My client Sergio is an overachiever, has always conquered his goals, and is extremely successful at the age of 36, but he had a baby nine months ago and has struggled to get back to his normal, overachieving state. "I just feel off, like I'm in a funk," he expressed to me.

He's doing what he's always done for the business, but as we unpacked things, I learned that his mornings feel out of his control. He isn't getting his values in as he did in the past, before the baby.

"I can't plan my day and attack it with consistency like I used to. I get up at 5:00 a.m. to organize my day and thoughts, but if the baby wakes up then, I'm on duty. I can't do my morning routine, and I feel scattered and disorganized. Sometimes I can plan out my day and feel prepared if she sleeps in, but if not, there's nothing I can do. The day doesn't get planned, and then I feel reactive all day just trying to get through."

I could hear the defeat in his voice as soon as he said there was nothing he could do. Victim! For an overachiever, not being able to achieve is like kryptonite. Even if the rest of their life is aligned, they still have a very keen sense of where they aren't achieving, and it will cause an upset in their life. And when they get into a victim mentality, they're powerless. Yes, the dynamics of

Sergio's life had changed, and he couldn't have this perfect morning to plan and strategize the day, but he'd fallen into the trap of thinking he had no choice. He was looking at this as if he only had two choices.

"So, you have no other options to plan your day if the baby is awake?" I asked.

He thought about what I'd said for a minute and laughed, "So, what you're saying is that I need to stop crying about it and figure out a different way."

He realized that he was being a victim and that it was taking away his ability to see other possibilities and set new intentions.

The next day I saw that he'd posted a picture of him planning out his day while his adorable baby bounced happily in front of him. Later that day, I received a text saying, "My day has been amazing." The only thing that changed in that twenty-hour time span was that he was now responsible for his actions and no longer a victim.

Pointing the finger at something or someone else isn't always intentional. Most of the time, you don't set out to be a victim; you just find yourself there. The key to realizing when you become a victim is being consciously aware of your thoughts so you can catch the moments when you're giving your power away.

It's easy to become a victim to the exact thing you're working so hard to create. I see this in the high-level people I coach. They've worked hard to build a thriving business and capture the success they always wanted, but it starts running them. My client Rebecca came to me after building her real estate business for ten years. She'd built a name and reputation for herself that she was proud of. She was making the money she wanted, but she was exhausted.

"I can't maintain this speed. I feel like I have to keep running at this pace in order for it to not all fall apart, but I can't do this for another twenty years. Something has to change," she said.

She was talking to clients late at night, and skipping her personal time for meditation and enjoying a slow morning because clients wanted to meet early. She'd built her business by doing whatever her clients needed her to do with no regard for her own values of family time, personal health, and peace and tranquility. She'd become a victim to her own business, and she felt trapped.

"What do you want it to be like?" I asked.

"I want to be able to start my morning with my meditation and not feel like I have to answer a call. I want to have dinner with my family without my phone on. I don't want to be on call so much," she replied.

"Okay, so what changes do you need to make to stop being a victim and take back your power?"

She just needed to give voice to where she'd lost her power and what she wanted to change. Then she could start making conscious choices that aligned with her values.

The new, empowered way you're living builds confidence and opens the door to start trusting yourself.

We can fall into the trap of giving away our power over our schedule and livelihood to others who don't even know the gravitas of us giving it away. You may plan to get breakfast with your partner in the morning, but you have a client scheduled on your calendar. You don't have to accept the booking, but you become a victim because you fear that if you say you can't make it and suggest another time, the client will be dissatisfied and may not refer business in the future. Trust me that when you make decisions based on your values, and stand in those choices without doubt, it will all work out in the best way. You need to trust other people to handle their emotions and their choices. Stop making up stories that people will be mad at you or send you a complaining email. Those stories are what put you in the victim zone. Are you willing to give up what's most important to you in an effort to try to control someone else's feelings? It's a lost cause, you can't do it. People have to own their emotions, and the sooner you acknowledge that, the better off you'll be. You get there by owning your own emotions first. When you take responsibility for your own feelings and stop making yourself a victim, it gets easier to create the space for others to handle their own emotions too. That's when it gets easier to step back and create the space for others to handle their own emotions too.

When you're living in a state of awareness, making conscious choices based on your values and controlling your thoughts, you're more likely to steer clear of a victim mentality. The new, empowered way you're living builds confidence and new intentions, and opens the door for you to start trusting yourself. Being able to say you fully trust yourself is a major component of living your best life in authenticity.

The Non-Negotiable You

- Takes ownership of their choices
- Creates what they want
- Learns from their mistakes

6

YOUR AUTHENTICITY

Ultimate freedom and the joy of starting with you are found through your authenticity. The highest goal is to be truly yourself and live your best life, not worrying about how you "should" show up. In the default life, being your true self is difficult because you don't have the control over your mind to shut down judgment and concerns from others. You perform as an ideal image for others based on habit and fear. You may also build your future based on fake confidence that works for other people but not for you.

With your new mastery of your mindset, you'll create space to step into your authentic self. When you start noticing that you feel good about your choices and decisions, whether big or small, you'll know that you've stepped onto the path of authenticity.

You need authenticity to make your contribution to the world and to your life. You've been created uniquely and have a gift to share, but it can only come from a place of personal acceptance and authenticity. Showing up authentically requires you to know without a doubt who you are. You may not have known before reading this, but you've been walking into your authenticity from the beginning of this book, learning your values, becoming conscious of your thoughts, and taking responsibility for your actions. As you continue building this relationship with yourself, you'll begin to trust yourself and have confidence in your authentic self. The non-negotiable you always shows up authentically.

If you don't know who you are, authenticity is impossible.

I ask people all the time, "What holds you back from being who you really are?" Fear of what other people think is the most common answer—when the reality is that most people don't know who they truly are, what they value, and what they want to create. It's that lack of self-awareness that keeps them from figuring out who they are, not other people's opinions of who they should be. For the most part, they don't set out to be inauthentic, they just find themselves lacking authenticity and wondering why.

Think about a close relationship that you have right now. Reflect on what it took to know that person well. You spent time with them and took an interest in learning about what they want and how they feel. That relationship was created through time, intention, awareness, commitment, consistency, trust, and honesty.

You need the exact same commitment to creating authenticity within yourself. When you have a close relationship with yourself, you know who you are and can find your authenticity. Rather than doubting who you are, you're never left wondering how to show up.

A new client named Bill gets nervous and uncomfortable around new people in meetings and events.

"What's behind that nervousness?" I asked.

"It's stressful trying to figure out quickly how I need to show up—what to say and how to act for that person."

I could hear his stress around trying to figure out how he should represent himself.

"So you're trying to figure out who they want you to be?" I confirmed.

"Yes. Everyone is different, so I need to show up differently depending on who they are."

"That's a big undertaking, trying to figure out how to show up and then being that person on demand," I reflected back to him.

I could hear he wasn't showing up as his authentic self, and this was creating two problems:

- You never know what someone else thinks without them telling you. Trying to figure out how they want you to show up is no more than a guess filled with assumptions and judgment.
- When you adjust to what you think the "right" version is, you subconsciously tell yourself that your authentic self isn't good enough.

"What makes you think you have to show up differently for each person you're meeting?" I asked.

"That's how I've been taught to get business, by being the person they want you to be," he said.

"I can understand why that would make you nervous. What would it be like to just be yourself?"

"I'm not sure I even know who that is, I've done this for so long."

I suggested we go back to his values to find some answers.

"So, who are you?" I asked, pressing on. He started with what he knew about himself from the basics, when he's with people he's comfortable around.

"I'm a kind person. I believe in God. I like to work hard and accomplish big goals. I love being outdoors and spending time with my family," he said.

We moved on to his intentions. He had the foundation of who he was, but he needed to nurture it through a relationship with himself. If you don't know who you are, authenticity is impossible. New awareness brings a tremendous amount of relief when you realize the new way will be much easier than the old way. His discovery was simple, it should've been obvious. Yet, this shows how we can get in our own way when we don't have a practice that allows us to see what's causing the obstacle.

"So I just need to show up as myself and stop trying to figure out who I should be?" he asked with relief in his voice.

Forgetting who you are prevents you from showing up authentically. Bill stopped worrying about how he showed up for people and showed up for himself. Before each meeting, he would remind himself of who he was and to just be that person. The nervousness became a thing of the past.

Authenticity holds your truest potential.

Worrying about what other people think can prevent you from showing up authentically. We spend a lot of time pretending to be someone we aren't, censoring our words and acting how we think we should, to obtain or hold on to success. It's as if you're telling yourself that you can't succeed by being your authentic self. This behavior is the antithesis of starting with you for your best life! The fear lies in how someone else will see you. Why do you care what people think of you? Because you've been basing your decisions and thoughts around their opinions, making the choice to abandon yours.

When you end up caring so much about what other people think, you create a filter for your own identity: When can I show up like me and when can't I? The harsh reality is that people's opinions of you are usually more about them, their self-judgment, and their insecurities. Here you are wasting emotional time and getting further away from your goals with every second you give to their opinion. If you had to choose your happiness and success or their opinion of you, which would you choose? When I give you the two options, it's a clear choice, right? But you're making decisions in contrast to that all day. Start giving yourself a choice. Your authenticity or their opinion, which is it going to be?

Authenticity holds your truest potential. This is how people unlock meaningful success and a life they love.

My client Suni had a business with the potential to skyrocket if she would let the world see who she really was; if she would show up and put herself out there, be herself, and be the thought leader she was.

"I want my business to grow. I want to put myself out there, but I'm terrified," she said. "What are people going to think? What are they going to say? Who am I to go out there? Who cares about what I have to say?"

"So you care about what people think of you?"

"No. I mean yes, I guess I do."

"What will happen if they don't like what you have to say?"

"Nothing, I guess. They don't work with me?"

"You don't *have* to do it. It's a choice you get to make. Just be sure you understand what you're choosing between," I told her. "You only get to pick one, is it your success and authenticity or the opinions of others? Which do you choose?"

"Well, when you put it that way, it's not much of a choice."

I got to see Suni gradually step out and become comfortable with being who she is. Her confidence increased, she began to trust herself, and, yes, her business took off. When we talk about it now, she laughs.

"I can't believe how worried I was to just be myself."

She wanted to show up and speak out about her talents and knowledge in her own authentic way, but she feared what people would think and what comments or negative feedback she would receive.

It takes courage and vulnerability to show up as your authentic self. You're basically saying, "Here I am; this is me. Take it or leave it." Don't give other people's opinions and judgments weight they don't deserve, and you don't change yourself into something other people want. If you let other people dictate how you show up, you'll get further and further away from your authentic self, making it more difficult to realize that you can be yourself.

Authenticity starts with knowing and accepting yourself.

I've had four people in the last year come to me for coaching for the same reason: they were playing roles that didn't sit well with who they really were, even though they were choosing to show up that way. One client named Mark, age 36, had built a whole business from an inauthentic place and was now completely tired of it. He was striving to get to retirement as a relief. He wanted to map out a plan to get there as fast as he could because he had grown tired of who he was pretending to be. I knew I had to first find out what had stopped him from being himself.

"I like my job," he said, "but I'm just tired of being someone I'm not. I have to dress a certain way, act a certain way, schmooze to get the deal. I'm over that! I just want to be me."

"What stops you from showing up as you and believing you'll have the success you want?" I asked.

"I don't know. I just have a work version of me that my clients expect."

Mark's work version was built from other people's expectations of him.

How many times have you created another version of yourself around a group, team, or social setting, showing a certain worth or value to be accepted? Showing up as someone different than you are every day to get a job done is exhausting. It could be eight hours a day that you're censoring what you say and how you act to show up as what you think someone needs to see. Not to mention the misalignment you create by attracting the wrong people. I dug in more with Mark about the process of going to work as himself instead of the work version.

"Is your personal version less of a quality person than your work version?" I asked.

"No, just different," he responded.

What helped in this session was that he had the awareness that he wasn't being true to himself, which made it easier to find other solutions besides retirement. He wasn't blaming others for how he had to be, he wasn't playing the victim. He was taking responsibility for his actions and making a change.

"What would it be like to just be the same you every day for anyone you associate with?" I asked him.

"That would be amazing."

At your core, in business and personal life, you should be the same person. You may have different roles and responsibilities, but you're still you! Authenticity starts with knowing yourself and accepting yourself. Your best life has you tuning in and listening to yourself every day, before anything else. It has you confidently taking the wheel and setting intentions for what you want to create based on your values. It has you affirming who you are and choosing your thoughts because you're the gatekeeper of your mind. And it has you being aware and honest to create the trust in yourself to be authentic all the time. It makes you the guide of your life instead of being guided by everything else around you. We get into trust more in-depth in the next chapter, but it's easier to trust yourself and be authentic when you show yourself how important you are every morning before anything else.

We don't set out to be inauthentic, it slowly happens over time. As soon as you start assessing how you should show up for people and how you find success, what they will like, and what will get you accepted, you start traveling down that road of losing your identity. It happens in our careers all the time, because you think you need to act the role of the job you have to fit that part.

Is there a difference between your work version and personal version? Take a piece of paper and write "Work" on the top-left and "Personal" on the top-right. Now start listing how that version of you shows up for each one.

Is there an opportunity to bring more of your authentic self to your work?

**Every time you show up as someone else,
you silently say you're not enough.**

When I started my career as a financial advisor, I was confident enough to accomplish anything, but that didn't mean I was authentic in the process. I hadn't gone to school to be a financial advisor, but the first job I had in my career was at Morgan Stanley. In fact, I didn't even have a four-year degree. I was shot down several times for the position because they required a four-year degree, but I was determined to get the job, mostly because I like to win. I was persistent, and I repeatedly told them it would be a great decision to hire me even though I had no experience or formal education in the investment world. I got the job, and after passing my securities license and going to training in New York for a few weeks, I was a licensed financial advisor—just like that. I was working in a male-dominated business at the age of 23 and had just made myself the only advisor in the office without a four-year degree. In my mind, I had to show up as someone else. I was already behind everyone else there, and I felt I'd better make up for the deficiency. I created a story that to get clients I had to be this polished, sophisticated, college-educated woman. I was extremely nervous, fearing the moment that someone would ask me where I went to college, so I convinced myself that I had to be serious and show up as someone I wasn't in order to prove that I was the best choice for their financial future.

I worked hard to prove to people that I was great at my role. And, honestly, I was, but I thought it was because of who I was showing up as. I sacrificed a lot of what was important to me to please other people and win in their eyes. I had an alter ego during the day. I did well, and I loved my clients and the business, but I changed into a different person when I was at home and could just be me. I was so busy being who I "needed" to be that I was losing myself in the process. What I didn't know then was that I could've been ten times as successful had I just been authentically myself. I wouldn't have worried about what people thought of me, and I wouldn't have made my decisions based on what other people wanted. I would've chosen what was best for me, which would've been the best for those I was serving. I would've been creating meaningful success and a life I loved from a place of authenticity.

Every time you show up as someone else, you silently say "I'm not enough," that you have to be something different to be accepted, valued, or liked. Over time, think about the impact that would have on your confidence. You'd get further and further away from your authentic self and your values. Eventually, you'd end up lost, questioning what makes you happy, wondering if you're in the right job, and asking, "What's my purpose?"

If you're letting that real, authentic version of yourself sit at home until you come back from work, you're holding yourself back from reaching your fullest potential and living your best life. You aren't giving people the opportunity to see you and connect with you.

Other people's feelings are not your responsibility. You don't get to control how they feel. When you stand in your authenticity in whatever profession you're in, you're truly unconcerned with what other people think about you. I don't mean that in a bad way, like you don't care about other people. Brace yourself for this: Not everyone is going to like you! Some of you are doubting me, but you're on an impossible mission if that's your goal. Trust me, I've tried. You end up with a lot of people who think you're nice and a good person, but very few real connections. You end up in the middle. You might think you're a master at being a chameleon, but where is your real identity? Get out of the middle, be you. Let people make their own choice whether they'll like you or not. It's okay if someone doesn't like you, you probably don't connect well with them anyway. Sometimes you don't realize that you're creating relationships with people you don't even care for.

Just because someone doesn't like you doesn't mean that you aren't an amazing human. You can be the greatest person and still have people that aren't going to like you. Accept that, and you'll feel the weight of the world come off your shoulders. That acceptance will open the door for you to be authentic. You can be confident about who you are and know that if someone doesn't accept you for that, it's okay. You can move on from having a relationship—business or professional—with them without any regret or fear. You aren't going to be everyone's cup of tea. Neither am I, and that's okay. For the ones that don't align with who you are, there will be twice as many who do, so make room for those people! But you have to be authentic in the way you present yourself to the world to find them. Your people will get you, connect to you, and bring more people into your life, both personally and professionally. Being your authentic self is like letting a giant exhale out that you've been holding in. You don't realize how hard it is to be inauthentic until you stop doing it. There's no turning back.

Your authentic self lives in abundance. No more scarcity about people not accepting you or missing out on events or business. You'll be so in love with what you do and how you show up that you'll attract the clients and people who are attracted to you. Look at your business and who you're attracting. If you don't love their energy and values, take a look at what you're bringing to the table. What you're representing is what you're drawing to yourself. If you're authentic, then you'll be attracting people and clients that align with you. But if you're showing up as someone you're not, you'll attract people and clients into your life on that false pretense and end up surrounding yourself with the wrong people. It's what you're welcoming.

The most important relationship you have is the one with yourself.

It's really hard to go out there and crush it if you aren't showing up as yourself every day and enjoying what you do. It's like trying to run a race with a boulder on your back. You get into paralysis and aren't taking action on anything because there's conflict and resistance. You're trying to motivate yourself to take action that isn't in alignment with who you are. How can you be motivated to do something that you truly want to stop doing? Major conflict and resistance are inevitable . You can't create meaningful success from a place of resistance. You have to take that boulder off your back to take the action that's going to create the success you've dreamt of. Then you'll find that you don't have to work so hard to achieve your goals and thrive in life.

My client Matt, head of sales for a finance company, recently got promoted and was facing imposter syndrome with fitting into his well-earned role. After some coaching around authenticity, he came back with an update.

"You know what's really cool? My boss told me he's really impressed with my leadership and the growth he's seen in me," he said.

"That's incredible! How does that make you feel?" I asked.

"It's great! But the funny thing is, I don't feel like I'm doing anything unique or special. I'm just being myself," he stated casually.

"You have arrived!" is what came to my mind for him. He had no idea how much power was in that statement. I couldn't help but smile ear to ear hearing his comment.

"What do you mean by that?" I asked. I wanted to create an awareness for him to hear what he was saying.

"I'm just being authentic and genuine. I'm trusting myself and not worrying about what others think. It's allowing me to be transparent and vulnerable," he said with pride.

"Sounds pretty unique and special to me," I replied.

If you'd like to take that glorious step of being authentic and free of fear of judgment, you need to know yourself. You get to know yourself by having a relationship with yourself, a relationship that you prioritize above everything because you're the one continual component of everything you do. Your job. Your marriage. Your career. Your friendships. Your health. Your growth. You bring yourself into all of these areas. The most important relationship you'll have is the one with yourself. It's critical that you have a relationship with yourself that you're committed to, an authentic relationship built on awareness, values, and honest intentions that you respect and are committed to. This can be the best relationship you've ever had because it's the only one you have total control over, the only relationship you can be 100 percent responsible for. Finding your authentic self is about knowing yourself, and it's all in your control. You don't have to rely on anyone else to make this relationship the best it can be. It's all yours if you're willing to build it.

We all have our moments of authenticity. For most people, those moments are when they're with family or close friends and trust they can be themselves. The reason we cherish the moments when we're completely ourselves is that they are few and far between. Wouldn't it be nice to live in those moments all the time? It starts with you choosing to spend time with yourself every morning before anything else. The time you take for yourself will bring your authenticity forward in all that you do. Once you show up authentically, you begin to trust yourself. And once you trust yourself, you become capable of anything you desire.

The Non-Negotiable You:

- Knows who they are
- Shows up as their true self
- Lives from their highest self

7

TRUSTING YOURSELF

Now that you're focused on living in a place of authenticity, you can start to trust yourself. How good does it feel to know the decisions you make and the outcomes you receive are based on being yourself? Trusting yourself is the central component of everything I'm teaching you. From when you wake up in the morning until you put your head on the pillow, trusting what matters to you most and acting on it is where you'll find peace. Living your life based on your values is going to require you to trust that you can choose the thoughts that will empower you to take action toward your goals. Trusting in yourself will also require staying clear of the victim mentality and taking responsibility for your actions. You can see that the commitments you keep, the awareness you have, and the choices you make will all rely on trusting yourself. Why? Because you're the best guide for yourself. No one knows you better than yourself!

Once you understand how your authentic self operates, following through on your commitments is the first major piece in building trust with yourself. Previous broken promises to yourself are big hurdles I see when it comes to clients trusting themselves. In the past, you may have been guilty of saying but not doing, but to be fair, you weren't operating from a place of authenticity then. You weren't aware or able to make conscious decisions based on your values. All the commitments you didn't keep to yourself before taught you to not trust yourself, so we have some rebuilding to do. Even if you don't think about it on a conscious level, in the back of your mind, you know there's a side door to sneak out of any time you commit to yourself, and your past behavior says you don't really have to do what you said you'd do.

You need to understand that you have the ability to follow through. You do it for other people all the time. Think about the commitments you make to others. If you said you'd meet a client, you're there. If you committed to meeting a valued family member or friend for lunch, you're there. There's no dropping that commitment because they're depending on you, they trust you. You show up for others from a place of trust and commitment, but you don't do the same for yourself. Imagine if you stayed committed and followed through with what you said you'd do for *yourself.* Your business would be more aligned with your values, and so would you. Your physical and mental health would reflect the love you have for your well-being. You'd trust yourself in all aspects of your life, not just showing up for others. If something did get in the way, you could trust that you have the awareness to learn from it and adjust for the next day. The non-negotiable you can trust your authentic, aware self to create meaningful success and a life you love!

Let's go after the low-hanging fruit first.

You are winning every day. Yes, you are, but you don't take the time to see it and celebrate it. Your mind goes to what you didn't do well enough or what you didn't get, but it forgets to look at what you *did* do. You can't build trust like that. How would that work in a relationship with someone, always focusing on what they didn't do and never acknowledging what they did do? Not a real trust builder. But again, you do that with yourself. Instead, imagine taking a minute every day to reflect on your win for the day.
Try it right now.

Where did you win yesterday? Make a list of even small wins, like getting out of bed and brushing your teeth. You did something to build trust within yourself. We take those little wins for granted and don't give ourselves credit, but when you use your awareness to acknowledge your wins, you build instant trust with yourself.

Building a deeper level of trust with yourself is easiest when you're in the present moment. We touched upon being present in Chapter Four on mindset. How present do you think you are on any given day? When I ask that question, most people say they very rarely feel present, maybe a two out of ten. If they aren't present, they're always steps ahead, worrying in a good or bad way about what's next. You can't trust yourself if you're always in the past with guilt or regret, or if you're in the future with fear and worry. It's not just the moments that you're taking action, it can even be the innocent times when you're driving and zone out, rethinking the mistake that you made or worrying about an upcoming challenge. Even those moments that feel like you aren't wasting time are affecting your self-trust. While you may have more control over your mind from your self-awareness, you can still fall into the trap of not trusting yourself in the present moment, especially if you've started to move toward a better life and more meaningful avenues to joy and success.

Worrying about the future will rob you of your self-trust.

I ask people all the time what holds them back from accomplishing their biggest dreams and goals, and it's always fear. Fear of all the unknowns. Will I succeed? Will I fail? What will people say? What will they think? Will I have a home to live in? Will I look like a fool? The list of fears goes on and on. None of those fears are here in the present moment, and they don't come from a place of authenticity. They're based on a lack of trust. Those limiting fears only live in the future within your mind. With control over your mindset, honesty with yourself, and self-awareness, you can trust that those fears are false and fabricated. You can find peace and trust right here in the beautiful present moment. When you go to the future to simply worry about something you don't have control over, you're creating your own fear and a lack of trust in yourself. You're contemplating outcomes without sufficient evidence.

The future holds unknowns. If you think too far forward into the future, you're putting yourself in a situation you aren't equipped for yet. The unknowns of the future can cause worry, anxiety, fear, and stress. If you're living there, it comes with all of those emotions. But when you trust yourself, you don't have to carry those emotions. You can find peace in the present.

I coach an intimate group of five go-getters. I started out coaching them every week on the core foundational pieces you've read in this book: values, awareness, mindset, and responsibility. They experienced a tremendous amount of growth and joy from the work they did. I slowly transitioned them to every other week and gave them space to fly a bit more independently. I felt they were in a place of authenticity where they could trust themselves.

There was reluctance. "I'm not so sure about this. I don't know if we're ready." They were ready. They needed to see that they could trust themselves. One week, there was a general consensus that they were experiencing more challenging dynamics.

"I'm aware of what's happening, but I still let a client get under my skin, and I'm not sure how to handle him," said one member.

"Yes, I'm aware. I see the doubt creeping in, but I'm not really doing anything about it," another member said.

"I really want to start training for a marathon, but I don't know. I'm not sure about it. I have a little anxiety over whether I can do it or not," said another participant.

The word *trust* was swirling in my head. They were all right there, in position to take the action, to lead themselves, but there was a lack of trust that had crept into their minds about their decisions and reactions. I started asking them one by one, "Do you trust yourself right here and now, in the present moment?"

Yes was the unanimous answer. I moved on to ask what each of them thought they needed to do with their respective situations, and they all had an answer. More proof that they could trust themselves. I wanted them to see what was causing the challenges they were experiencing on their own, so I asked, "What was making this difficult for you on your own?"

"I was worried about failing."

"I was worried about how the guy would react or what he would think."

"I was worried about what other people might think of me."

The thoughts of the future were robbing them of their self-trust in the present moment. Why else would they have all that worry? They were all thinking about the future, with all of its unknowns and uncontrollable variables. I encouraged each of them:

"Respond to the client based on your values, because that's what guides you."

"Set daily intentions to train for that marathon and trust you'll be ready when the time comes."

"Show up as yourself and let go of what others think because your authenticity has shown you who you are."

Worrying about the future will rob you of your self-trust. In the present moment, you can trust yourself and make a conscious decision that aligns with your values and confidence. Do the work for you to trust yourself.

Your past experiences don't define you.

When you trust yourself, you don't have to keep reliving and regretting moments from the past. As I mentioned with authenticity, the act of living with regret is a barrier to making conscious decisions that align with your best life. You may have made some bad choices when you weren't aligned with your values, but that's over. You can simply move on, learn a lesson, and make different decisions, but not if you're still in the past. I find this is a nervous habit of people who are prone to living in the past and don't want to step into trusting that they've done the work.

When my client Desiree first came to me, she had a habit of beating herself up for past mistakes. She would send herself in a downward spiral for days, derailing her off the path of success.

"I just get so mad at myself when I make a stupid mistake. I keep replaying it over and over again, trying to bang it into my head so that I don't do it again."

The emphasis she put on banging it into her head clued me in that she was afraid she would forget it.

"What's the goal around banging it into your head?" I asked.

"I don't want to make the same mistake again."

"What makes you think you will?"

"I don't know, I just want to make sure!"

"Do you trust yourself not to make the same mistake again?"

She had to think about it but, eventually, decided, "Yes, I do. I've thought about how I could avoid the same thing in the future. I've even created checks and balances to make sure it doesn't happen again."

As she continued to share her process and plan, she said, "Okay, that feels better. I feel like a weight was just lifted off me."

It was the acknowledgment of trust she gave herself that freed her from the past. She was only stuck there because she didn't know that she could trust herself not to make the same mistake again.

Your past experiences don't define you. You can't believe that you're going to repeat the same behavior. Now, in the present moment, you're different. You know your values, you can control your mind, and you can make conscious choices. You have tools and a relationship with yourself that you can trust. You've seen the difference when you make decisions from an authentic place. You don't need to punish yourself, again and again, to make sure a mistake doesn't happen. You're self-aware, you learn from your mistakes, and can confidently move on because you have a different relationship with yourself that you can trust now.

We've all made poor decisions in the past. Over time, repeated poor decisions create a lack of trust in your abilities to lead yourself. If you aren't in control of your mind, you'll let your old stories and patterns convince you that you are not trustworthy. I want you to change that story. Back then, your decisions were based on feelings and lacked a conscious mind. Now you're making conscious decisions based on your values. It's a different process with a drastically different result. Being able to control your mind to make decisions that serve you leads to self-trust.

Trust in yourself is not trusting that you'll be perfect.

You can trust yourself and still fail. Trusting yourself is not about being right 100 percent of the time. I asked my client Cori if she trusted herself.

"Not all the way. I don't trust that I'll always make the right decision."

I heard instantly that she was basing her trust on perfection. Those are unrealistic expectations for anyone.

"Does anyone always make the right choice?"

"I don't know, maybe not."

"I certainly don't. We're going to make the wrong choice sometimes, it's how we learn and grow. But can you trust that you'll be aware and capable of leading yourself through it either way?"

"*Yes!*"

That's all the trust she needs. Trust in yourself is not trusting that you'll be perfect, it's about trusting yourself to navigate the ups and the downs, the wins and the losses, the joys and the sorrows. The self-awareness that you live with every day helps you retain that trust in yourself. You aren't turning a blind eye to what you know you need or might be falling short in, you're committed to being aware and honest every day. You start to see your missteps as opportunities to grow instead of terrible failures because your expectations are to do your best, not be perfect. Letting go of perfection opens the door for you to trust your actions, not your results.

You have to believe and trust that your actions will create what you want even if there are failures first. You know how to choose your thoughts and control your mind by reframing any doubtful thoughts into learning experiences you can trust.

In the past, you might've had doubtful thoughts like:

"Why did I call that person?"

"I should've known that deal would fall through."

"I should've been a better judge of character."

Trust in yourself can change those doubtful thoughts into growth opportunities that sound like:

- "What can I learn from this call?"
- "What could I have done to save the deal?"
- "What should I be aware of when working with people in the future?"

Be vigilant about choosing thoughts that will continue to show you trust yourself, even when it feels like the odds are against you. It's a magical moment when you can find peace and trust that the outcome you get is all part of the plan, whether it leads to your desire now or later.

Faith is what gives you trust in what you can't control.

Trusting what's in your control becomes achievable with the work you're doing on yourself. You gain control of your actions, your thoughts, and your choices. Your trust in controlling these comes quickly when you're showing up for yourself every day and practicing what you've learned. It's when you face variables you *can't* control that you're going to need something bigger than yourself to trust in. As you learned in Chapter Four, you can't control other people's thoughts, feelings, actions, and choices. Your continued efforts to try to control what you can't will jeopardize your authenticity and keep you in a state of worry. You need a place to surrender all that you can't control.

I'm not here to lead you down a spiritual journey. You have to make that decision on your own, but I can tell you that having faith in something bigger than yourself goes a long way in dealing with the uncontrollable and trusting yourself. As you learn and accept what isn't yours to control, you open up space to let something bigger in. That bigger component is what you put your faith in. For me, it's God, but maybe it's something different for you. Maybe it's fate, the universe, destiny, divine intervention, whatever is right for you, but you need to believe in something bigger than yourself to surrender what you're not responsible for, what you can't control. Faith is what gives you trust in what you can't control.

When I start working with a new client, I ask them to rate their level of spirituality. I know it's a broad question, but I intend it to be that way to give my clients the space to make it what they want. I'm not here to judge if they have a relationship with a religion or pull tarot cards every morning, I'm simply wanting to know if they believe there is anything bigger than themselves playing a role in their life. It's a good indication of whether or not they're carrying the entire weight of the world on their back. Without fail, the clients that don't have a belief in anything are trying to control everything and don't trust the outcome with their authentic selves. It's an impossible task, and it causes exhaustion and defeat. Eventually, as they do the work we've discussed in the first six chapters, they come to a place of trusting themselves to handle what they're responsible for while recognizing that everything else needs to be surrendered. Daily prayer is that place to dump what you can't control so you can move forward without the burden of worry. Asking for guidance, requesting an outcome, or simply handing over what's too heavy to carry can be prayer. There's a great deal of peace when you trust that someone or something else bigger than you has you covered.

Gratitude creates trust in your faith.

Just like with building trust in yourself, you also need to build trust in your faith. There's a tremendous amount of trust needed to accept the idea that some situations and outcomes unfold exactly the way they're supposed to, even if it isn't how you wanted. You can build that trust every day by acknowledging how your faith or the universe showed up in your life. We don't often give credit to what's bigger than us, which prevents us from believing and trusting in our faith. If you don't give credit where credit is due, how do you believe and trust that power? Gratitude creates trust in your faith. When you give credit, such as gratitude, to what's bigger than you, it creates a confirmation and belief that builds trust in your faith. Over time, that trust becomes so powerful that you're able to find gratitude for what you might perceive as unfortunate, acknowledging that it's all part of a plan you can trust. Daily gratitude is the practice of recognizing and being grateful for what faith has handed you, while prayer is the place to surrender what you can't control.

Ditching fear of the unknown comes with the trust you're building. The trust you have in yourself will stop you from projecting yourself into the future where the unknown lives. When you combine that self-trust with trust in your faith, you can turn the unknown from fearful into exciting. The unknown becomes one of those grab-bags you got and couldn't wait to open. Every single day, your gratitude and prayer acknowledge and surrender to what's supposed to be. You find peace in the unknown because you trust that whatever life gives you, it's from you showing up authentically, seeking out your desires, and living your values. With this trust, you're ready to start creating meaningful success and a life you love. You have the foundation from the first seven chapters, and now, I'm going to give you the tool to set you up for daily success with the Morning Mindset. What you read and learned is only as good as what you do with it. When you implement all that you've learned into a daily fifteen-minute practice, you integrate your new habits and mindset into your life. Staying on this path leads you to create meaningful success and a life you love.

The Non-Negotiable You:

- Trusts themself
- Honors self commitment
- Surrenders the uncontrollables

8

THE MORNING MINDSET

We've taken a hard, honest look at the core of what it takes to be the best you—your values, self-awareness, choices, mindset, responsibility, authenticity, and trust. If what you've been learning resonates and you want this new limitless life, I'm going to show you how it's built on a daily basis. All that I've been teaching you comes together into a morning ritual—the Morning Mindset—that will consistently build your self-trust and a better life in an effective way. One day, after time with this practice, you'll find yourself saying, "I'll never go back to the person I once was." This happens quicker for some people than others, but everyone has the realization that how they were once operating no longer makes any sense. They can't imagine a day where they don't start with themselves first. I'm not asking you to be selfish, just to take care of yourself so you can help others from the best version of yourself.

Everything you've learned up until now will make absolute sense once you start doing the Morning Mindset practice every day. This morning routine will bring to life all the wonderful pieces of you we've been discovering and exploring. Building a relationship of awareness with yourself and creating trust, consistency, confidence, responsibility, and presence are all encompassed in this routine. All I need from you now is intentional action and a commitment to yourself to strive for the best life and leave any remnants of the default life behind.

You are the creator of the life you want to live, so it's your responsibility to step into that role every morning before you do anything else. Whether you want a peaceful, stress-free life, or you want to tap into your full potential, you can have what you choose when you show up for yourself every day in the Morning Mindset. There are no excuses and no one to blame if you don't take advantage of the opportunity you have to live authentically in your best life.

As we learned in Chapter Four, as soon as you wake up, your mind is off and running. You have to grab hold of your thoughts before you start tuning in to everyone else around you. The practice of the Morning Mindset will focus your mind by shaping your thoughts before the day even starts. Imagine if you did all you wanted and hoped for in your day. That would feel fantastic, right? You can have a day of your making when you start it with you first! When you take an inventory of how you're waking up and the thoughts that dominate your mind, you're telling yourself, "I'm worth the time to reset and will honor the way I'm heading into this precious day." You're the most important piece of the puzzle in your life. If you tune in to emails, clients, social media, and news first, you're saying that the noise of other people is more important than your thoughts; that the opinions or perceptions of others are more important than grounding yourself in your intentions for your day.

The success you crave, whether it's financial, creative, or spiritual, will find you naturally when you put yourself first. When you put the needs of other people before your needs first thing in the morning, you're choosing a reactive, less effective day. Tuning in to your relationship with yourself first every morning is imperative to creating meaningful success and your best life. Let me ask you this: What do you need to have a great relationship with someone? Most people answer that you need honesty, trust, commitment, authenticity, and dependability. Now, rate all of those pieces when it comes to the relationship you have with yourself. Would you say it's a great relationship? I don't mean how you rate yourself in those areas with other people, I mean how are you with yourself? Chances are, when you make a commitment with someone else to be somewhere, you'll follow through. How about when you commit to yourself, are you always there?

Your goal here is to have the best relationship with yourself consistently. One that sets the standards for all your relationships. How do you do this, you ask? You show up every day for yourself by taking fifteen minutes in the Morning Mindset practice to direct your mind to get in the driver's seat and own your day. You take that time to get into the best frame of mind. You set intentions for making the day unfold as you wish. You take all the foundational work we've done in Chapters One through Seven and apply them in the Morning Mindset. You show gratitude and create abundance and ask for what you want because you can have it! You'll be able to notice sooner when you're off track—when what's unfolding isn't in alignment with the intentions and desires you wrote for the day. No more being surprised at what did or didn't get done. Rain or shine, busy or not, stressed or calm, working or on vacation, when you do the Morning Mindset, you show up for yourself—every day, in a routine way, and without stopping. Setting your mind up for success is the most important job you have!

Sometimes clients will ask, "How long do I do this? Do I do it forever?" The answer is yes, forever. You don't have to, but you'll want to. Change your mindset around the finality of "forever." Thankfully, you learned in Chapter Four how to effectively choose your thoughts. You could think of this as a burden or view it as a privilege. You get the privilege of having a relationship with yourself that will create your best life in a simple, fifteen-minute-a-day routine.

My client Daniel was struggling with creating better habits and disciplines for his day. He wanted more success in his business and a healthier lifestyle, but he wasn't following through with what was most important to him.

I had previously asked him to do the Morning Mindset, but when I asked him about the results, he said, "It feels like a chore, like I have to do this."

"You don't *have* to do the Morning Mindset," I told him. "Having to do something defeats the purpose. You're putting yourself right back into a victim mentality. You have a choice here. You get to choose if you want to create the day you want, or get stuck with the day that you get."

Understanding that it's a choice was the shift for him. He started choosing to do the Morning Mindset to create the day he wanted. It took him over six months to do it consistently. When he came to my office at the end of the six months, he was elated. "I have so much love for myself. I don't get mad at what happens to me anymore. I'm getting so many deals, business is abundant, and I have so much more joy in new experiences. It's amazing. I get to take this time for myself every morning, and it feels life-affirming!"

You, too, can create what you want by making note each morning of who you are and what you want through intention, affirmations, gratitude, and prayer. You can check back with your values and goals and confirm whether what you're creating each day matches your Morning Mindset. You can then show up for yourself daily with a strong commitment to what you want in your life. You'll have increased confidence and intention, making pursuing your goals and living life more enjoyable.

Creating this daily routine is just as important as the other health routines you have in your life. You brush your teeth every day or else they would look terrible, your breath would stink, and your teeth would rot. Significant consequences, agreed? You eat every day to fuel your body or else you wouldn't survive—you would be malnourished, hangry, and you wouldn't be able to keep going. Again, big consequences. You sleep every night to rest and recover your body or else you wouldn't be able to function, no choice there. But what about your mindset? Unfortunately, people tend to deny the consequences of not taking care of their minds or put little emphasis on the value until they're at rock bottom—anxious, depressed, and stressed out. Then they take notice! Managing stress, anxiety, overwhelm, doubt, depression, guilt, lack of joy, unfulfillment, powerlessness, and reactiveness are just as important as brushing your teeth or eating. You don't have to face the consequences of a mismanagement of your mind, you can create a daily habit that will fuel your mind and create meaningful success and a life you truly *love*!

You might be thinking, "I have a great morning routine. I check my emails, then I make breakfast and hang with the kids, then I walk my dog and head to work. I don't have time for much else." Yes, that's a morning routine, and I want you to keep those great habits, but I want you to insert this Morning Mindset routine before all those other great actions. I'm talking about a routine that gets you in the right frame of mind before your daily routine, one that works on your mind to prepare you for the day you're creating!

When you show up for yourself every day, you get to know yourself, which builds trust and authenticity. Trusting in your authenticity keeps you present and gets you over every hurdle; it's the biggest game-changer for my clients. Once people hit their stride with trust in themselves, their lives change. The results are different for everyone, but initially, it fills the areas that you need most.

I receive texts all the time from clients about how simple the Morning Mindset is and that when they're consistent with it every morning, business comes easy and life is less stressful. They choose the daily habit of the Morning Mindset because it keeps them from falling into old patterns. When they show up for themselves, their values get met and they feel fulfilled. They don't allow their minds to get hijacked by other people's opinions, they stay in the present, in control of what they're responsible for.

Carrie, who initially came to me because she was overwhelmed and stressed from juggling the demands of being a business owner, wife, and mother, wanted peace and order in her life. I got her started on the Morning Mindset, which she embraced, but a month later she came back to me frazzled.

"I was doing so good. Business was great and my days were so calm and manageable. But then I slipped up on my Morning Mindset."

"What caused the slip-up?"

"I just felt like I was doing really good and wanted to get a jump on some other things I'm working on."

"How did that go for you?"

"Not good! I'm stressed again. It feels like I have too much to do and not enough time. I'm reactive and snippy."

"So what do you need to do?"

"Just get back to the Morning Mindset. Tomorrow."

I simply redirected her back to the Morning Mindset practice that was bringing her peace and order. The very next day, she texted: "I'm back, thank you!" When you trust your choices, it's easier to get back on the path to success. You know what you need because you've been in a pattern of awareness and adjustment as your authentic self.

From the beginning of this book, I've been introducing you to the pieces you need to be your best self, live your best life, and create your greatness. Looking at each of those chapters, it might seem overwhelming to think you have to be aware, live your values, master your mindset, take responsibility, show up authentically, and trust yourself every day, but it isn't if you use the Morning Mindset. This daily practice was designed to give you the space to work on all of those growth areas in fifteen minutes a day. Commit to yourself for one hundred days, use your values, and set a goal. This is your time to show up for yourself! You are worth it, and you deserve it. Take this leap and trust yourself to do it. What do you have to lose?

The Morning Mindset

Anyone can do this eight-step routine anywhere. All you need is a pen and paper. I have a printable worksheet for free that you can use to do the Morning Mindset (see QR code at the end of this chapter), or you can use your own notebook or my companion journal that has the practice outlined for you. If you decide to use your own notebook, you can simply write out the eight steps below. Set yourself up for success by having it ready to go every morning. Have the journal set out, the sheets preprinted, or your notebook ready with prompts.

Here we go!

AWARENESS

I feel...

1. "I feel" (awareness): The first step of the Morning Mindset is to understand how you feel by creating awareness. When you ask yourself how you feel, you're acknowledging yourself and giving yourself an opportunity to be honest. In that moment, you're present and using your conscious mind. Remember that in Chapter Three we learned that awareness gives you the knowledge to change and grow. It's imperative that you create awareness with yourself so you aren't stuck being a victim of how you feel. You have to know how you feel to change your state of mind. It can be tempting to shove those feelings down and turn a blind eye, but you take your power away when you do that. Too often people move through the day with no awareness of how they feel or what they can change. They operate on autopilot and just take what they get. They're in the beginning stages of victim mentality. If you start your day checking in with yourself, you create awareness.

Write down what the feelings are, and keep it simple.

You don't need to write an essay about your feelings or a long story about who caused those feelings. It's a simple assessment and acknowledgment of the present moment. You're being honest and truthful with yourself in a simple way and being heard. Don't be afraid to acknowledge how you really feel, because you get to change it! The only wrong answer is an untruthful one. So, how do you feel?

- I feel stressed.
- I feel overwhelmed.
- I feel exhausted.
- I feel excited.
- I feel good.

Watch out for surface answers that may pop up like "fine" or "sleepy." You might feel these on the surface, but dig a little deeper and ask yourself if there's anything else you're feeling.

As you start consistently acknowledging and being aware of your morning thoughts, you'll see that your awareness starts to head in a different direction. All of a sudden, you're writing down the words *great, good, focused,* or *excited* to describe how you feel! This is a normal progression for two reasons. One, because the Morning Mindset is changing your days and your mind. Two, because your mind starts to shift out of the default thoughts, knowing you have the power to choose differently and do something about it; you aren't a victim to them anymore.

When you first start this section of the Morning Mindset, you may experience these common reactions:

- "I'm always writing down tired, am I doing it right?"
- "I don't even know how I feel first thing in the morning."

- "I find myself always writing down something negative."
- "I feel like I'm searching for something, but nothing is coming up."
- "I feel like I don't want to write anything negative and give energy to it."

"Tired," for example, can be a reaction to the way you feel out of habit. If you wake up stressed, try writing down your honest thoughts, like, *I don't feel like working today.*

Your feelings will evolve and change when you give them the space to be heard, and you can then access new feelings of excitement and happiness.

ADJUSTMENTS

I can... _____

2. "I can" (adjust): Now that you have awareness of how you feel, in the second step, you can make adjustments if needed to change your feelings and get into your optimal zone. Your optimal zone is the best mindset to make decisions and take actions that align with your values. We want you to create your day from your optimal zone to bring your best self into the day. In Chapter Four, I explained that you are not your feelings. You have the power to change your feelings by choosing different thoughts and actions. This is your opportunity to change the way your feelings will affect your day. You can make a change in this moment to how you feel, which will affect the way you show up. Ask yourself, "What can I do to change the way I feel?" Your adjustment might be a change of thought, or it could be an action. If you feel stressed or worried, you can choose a thought that will change your feelings. If you feel overwhelmed, your adjustment might be to make a list to prioritize and get back into your optimal space. If you feel tired, you might stand up to stretch and breathe. Or your action could be to have more espresso. Initially, you might feel like you don't have an answer; it's normal to feel like a victim of your feelings when you start. Even if you don't think your answer is great, you're showing yourself that you care, and that effort will create growth. Eventually, you'll feel more empowered, and you'll see that you are your best guide in redirecting yourself. You'll learn what serves you and will get to know yourself on a deeper level. As time passes, the actions you take may evolve into something upper-level that is more aligned with your values like, *I need a walk in nature*. This is a big moment of self-awareness.

Write down one action you can take
to get into the optimal zone.

There is no right or wrong answer, so don't judge yours. Just use your conscious mind to think, "What would change these feelings for me?" Don't be pressured to find the perfect answer here, you might not have it. I know you can come up with something, and that something is action that will navigate you away from the feelings that aren't serving you. It's about you becoming present in the moment and serving yourself, and doing something with the awareness that you just created in the first step. Tell yourself, "I can adjust to get to my optimal zone by..." For example:

- I feel stressed. I can adjust by staying in the present moment and focusing on what I need to do right now.
- I feel overwhelmed. I can adjust by making a list of what I need to do and prioritizing it.
- I feel exhausted. I can adjust by taking a few minutes to stretch, having a ten-minute walk outside, or getting to bed earlier this evening.

As you build a relationship with yourself through consistency and commitment to this daily practice, you'll start to trust yourself, and your answers will become more valuable and creative. You'll love this opportunity to serve yourself with what you need!

INTENTIONS

I will...

1. ....

2. ....

3. ....

4. ....

5. ....

3. "I will" (intentions): After you've assessed how you feel and made any necessary adjustments to get into your optimal zone, you're ready to create the day you want with step three: setting your intentions for the day and writing them down. Your intentions are not a never-ending to-do list of everything that needs to get done. As we discussed in Chapter Five, your intentions and values hold weight and meaning, they give you the opportunity to build confidence in yourself by staying committed to your word. Go back to Chapter Two on values and reread how important it is to live your values to fuel yourself and live your best life. Some values show up organically in your day-to-day life, but others you have to intentionally make happen.

The intentions you set are actions you'll take to get you closer to your goals and living your values. This process sets you up to be proactive about where your time goes. It puts you in the driver's seat so you have a say about what goes on in your day. Intentions also give you confirmation that you had a productive day and not just a busy one. It'll be easier to wind down at the day's end and take comfort in knowing you did what you intended.

Your intentions might be a particular to-do item, or they might involve how you show up for your day. Regardless of the intentions you set, you should be committed to following through—it's not a to-do list full of maybes. When you set your intentions and follow through, you build your confidence in your ability to create and conquer the day you want. The repeated success you encounter will lead to you believing and going after your true desires.

Write down a few intentions for your day.

Think about what you want to have in your day. What do you want to accomplish? How do you want to show up? This is where you get a say in your day! Set intentions you'll be proud to accomplish and feel good about at the end of the day. For example:

- I will spend an hour connecting with past clients.
- I will write for 30 minutes.
- I will go to an exercise class.
- I will choose peace.
- I will be present.
- I will sit outside for lunch and enjoy the present moment.
- I will put my phone away in the evening.

No matter what you do, your intentions should align with your values and goals. It's up to you what intentions you set, but remember, you're creating the day you order up, so choose wisely.

AFFIRMATIONS

I am... _____

_____

_____

4. "I am" (affirmation): When I bring up affirmations to people, they either say, "Oh, I love affirmations, I do them every morning!" or I get an eye roll. I confess: I was an eye-roller a long time ago. Affirmations seemed a little too "woo-woo" for me, but I can admit that I was wrong. In step four, you'll state affirmations to confirm who you're calling yourself to be. You learned in Chapter Four that your thoughts create your feelings. When you write your affirmations, you're feeding your mind the thoughts you want it to operate with. Therefore, using affirmations builds confidence, gives acknowledgment, feeds the mind, and forges a path, but they're only valuable if you use them right. You can't just say some outlandish affirmations, sit back, and expect miracles to happen. If you're spending time with yourself every morning, being honest, creating awareness, and setting intentions and acting on them, the affirmations that you need to empower you to honor your values and goals will speak for themselves. If you're looking to position yourself as a leader in your field and you're concerned about how you stack up to the competition, an affirmation could be, *I am a leader in my industry.*

Tell your mind what you want it to believe by writing out five to seven affirmations. For example:

- I am patient.
- I am focused and disciplined.
- I am present and intentional in my actions.
- I am a best-selling author.
- I am grateful.
- I am enough.

Recognize and acknowledge who you're affirming yourself to be. Writing out your affirmations builds your confidence and helps you to step into who and what you're creating. Your affirmations become daily reminders, and they can be specific to the intentions you just set. If you want to take an hour to call past clients, your affirmation could be, *I am a caring and thoughtful connector. I am genuinely curious about my clients.* You can also choose constant affirmations to remind yourself of who you are or who you want to be. I have a few affirmations that always show up for me: *I trust myself* and *I choose my thoughts.* When you're checking in with yourself every morning, you'll start to know what you need because the same affirmations will keep showing up.

REVIEW: As you flow from step one to step four in the Morning Mindset, you'll see how this process all connects. For example, if in the first step if you wrote, *I feel nervous about a presentation I have to give,* your "I can" statement might be, *I can adjust by keeping my mind in the present moment.* Then, when you move to your intentions, they might be *Thirty minutes of preparation for the presentation, five minutes of breath work,* *staying present*, and *trusting myself*. Then you start writing your affirmations, and they could come out as, *I trust myself*, *I live in the present moment*, *I am calm*, *I am a powerful presenter*, and *I captivate audiences.*

Can you see all the intention and power you're harnessing? You're taking control of your day! It isn't always specific to one event, and there's no right or wrong. It's about trusting yourself to set your day up and be intentional about what you want.

GRATITUDE

I'm grateful for... _____

_____

_____

5. "I'm grateful" (gratitude): Daily gratitude is underrated! It contributes a tremendous amount of value to your life. It goes beyond saying "I'm thankful for a roof over my head," or "I'm thankful for my health." Yes, all true, but that's just the tip of the iceberg. If you stick to the same surface-level gratitude list day in and day out, you're missing the greater benefits of daily gratitude. Lip service is a rinse and repeat cycle that doesn't do a whole lot. In step five of the Morning Mindset, in order for your gratitude to be a mind-opener and perspective-changer, you also need to be grateful for what you don't have yet and for difficulties and challenging situations. Being grateful for pleasant things is easy, but you create opportunities for growth by appreciating what, at face value, could be a problem. Gratitude enables you to see more sides of the circumstance.

In Chapter Five, we discussed how being a victim gives your power away, and the same goes for gratitude. If you can't find gratitude in unfavorable circumstances, you're giving your power away. Challenge your mind to find the gratitude in situations that the default mind would view as negative. You get to expand your mind beyond what isn't ideal. In the default mindset, losing a client might create a victim mentality and send you into making choices that don't align with your values. Now, with the Morning Mindset, you might look at losing a client as an opportunity to set better boundaries, increase your fees, or have more time to live your values. Reframing an experience creates gratitude and opportunities for the mind. Looking over the previous day and finding gratitude in the moments that might have escaped you helps you keep a positive mindset going forward.

Reflect for a minute and write down four to six moments you're grateful for. For example:

- The birds woke me up.
- The smile on my loved one's face.
- The laugh I shared with a friend.
- The canceled appointment that created time for myself.

The gratitude and joy around those moments help you slow down to be present in these experiences as they occur.

PRAYER

I'm asking for... _____

_____

_____

_____

6. "I'm asking for" (prayer): Prayer is a critical piece to the Morning Mindset. In this sixth step, you get to ask for what you want. This is the place where you can rely on a power bigger than yourself to take away the burden of the uncontrollable variables that are taking up precious bandwidth. The stress and anxiety people typically experience come from a lack of control over a particular issue or outcome. Some people can simply choose to not think about the things they can't control, but for others, it's not that simple. Being able to give the uncontrollable up to someone or something is a powerful practice. That someone or something might be the universe, fate, God, the cosmos, whatever you choose, but have that bigger-than-you place to give your worries to, because you need to put out there what you would like to see happen for you in the day. This is not wishful thinking, but rather leaning on your spirituality and faith, trusting that you have a partner with a force greater than your own. It takes courage to be brave and ask for what you want, and there's an element of deserving it that comes into play. When you're showing up for yourself every morning and doing the work, you do deserve it! So ask for it, pray for it!

Write down what you're asking for or what uncontrollable variables you're handing over. For example:

- I pray you keep my family safe and healthy.
- I pray you give me peace to not worry about the things I can't control.
- I pray you put people in my path that I can help and serve.
- I pray you help me see the next steps in growing my business.
- I pray you give Sarah the courage to speak up about her value and worth.

Your prayers might be about you or someone else. Mine are often around my clients, a loved one, or even a stranger on the street. That energy and faith I'm putting out there make a difference, and when you start to see the results, it brings joy and gratitude. Enlist the support of a higher power to multiply your efforts and your results. Through prayer, meditation, or other spiritual connections, you send a message of what you want to create and receive.

VISUALIZATIONS

I see...

_____

_____

_____

7. "I see" (visualization): You've heard the saying "seeing is believing," and that's what I want you to do here in step seven. Muhammad Ali said, "If my mind can conceive it and my heart can believe it, then I can achieve it." You've just adjusted to get into your optimal zone, you've set your intentions and fed your mind affirmations. Now it's time to see the day you want. We've already established how powerful the mind is, so use that to your advantage. What you've laid out for your day comes from a place of honesty and authenticity. Trust that and create the vision that will bring it to life. This is science, not hocus-pocus. When you visualize doing something, it sends a message to your brain to perform that action. The visualization becomes a rehearsal, and your brain believes it's actually taking the action again and again. This process creates confidence and reduces stress. If your mind thinks you've already done something, you'll be more confident in taking that action and less stressed about the execution. Professional athletes use visualization all the time to see themselves winning—they visualize the shot and picture themselves scoring. You can use the same technique when visualizing your day.

Take a minute or two to visualize your day and write that visualization down. For example:

- I see a peaceful day of sticking to my schedule and running on time.
- I see my client shaking my hand, smiling and excited to start working together on their new deal.
- I see a focused day of creating content and feeling accomplished.

- I see a calm and joyful day of being present and connecting with people on a deeper level.
- I see myself speaking confidently in front of a room full of people. I see them nodding and acknowledging what they're learning.

You know what lies ahead, so how do you want to see it play out? Do you have a busy day that seems a little overwhelming? Change that thought to a positive vibration by visualizing a smooth flow to the day. Sometimes it's something specific, like visualizing how one important sales call will go. How do you visualize this experience turning out? Do you see yourself talking with the potential client, connecting, and laughing? Shaking their hand and welcoming them as a new client? You should if that's what you want. If you leave it up to the default mind, you'll be missing an opportunity to visualize what you want to create.

You just completed the most meaningful ten to fifteen minutes of the day for yourself. What I just laid out for you is the simplest yet hardest thing you'll ever do. The Morning Mindset will reroute you from the default life to your best life. This simple process will bring you closer to yourself than you've ever been, giving you the ability to create whatever you want in your life. It won't be an overnight miracle, so be prepared to stick with it. This isn't a quick fix that will lose its luster, this is a new way of living, one you won't want to turn away from.

The Non-Negotiable You

- Proactively creates their day
- Prioritizes themself
- Guides themself

The Morning Mindset Worksheet

9

YOUR MORNING MINDSET EVERY DAY

Consistency is the key when working with the Morning Mindset. Start showing up for yourself every morning; notice how you feel, what you can affirm about yourself, and your intentions, gratitude, and prayers, you'll begin to see a consistent difference in your day. If you're prone to impatience, now is the time to trust the process, even when you wake up not feeling optimal. Once you start, you'll get instant gratification like pride and accomplishment from showing up for yourself. You'll be more productive and calm and less stressed. At first these feelings alone might be enough to motivate you each morning. But if that starts to feel like calm and accomplishment alone are not enough, just stick with the practice. With consistency and fortitude, you will soon see the real dividends of the practice start to pay. When you commit to making the Morning Mindset the start of your day, every day—before email, before the kids, and cutting off the monkey mind before it gets whirling—you'll witness a whole new version of yourself emerge.

Clients routinely point out that I'm calm, and they ask how I got that way. This is the way! I wasn't always calm—far from it, actually. As you saw from my time as a financial planner, I was reactive and controlling. I based so much of what I did on other people's feelings and expectations of me. I put myself in last place because I thought it was better to take care of everyone else first. The calmness and joy came from deeply knowing myself and starting with myself first every day. Today, I trust the decisions I make, take responsibility for my actions and thoughts, and am present and aware of who I am and what I'm doing. Once you commit to showing up consistently for yourself every day, you can feel the same way. It's not complicated; there's no magic solution. You create the life you want to live, all day, every day, through your Morning Mindset practice.

Now that you've learned and experienced the seven steps of the Morning Mindset, I would be doing you a disservice if I didn't make you aware of potential pitfalls. The first obvious downfall is the start-and-stop experience. You'll notice a change; you'll feel more at ease and in control of your day and believe you're doing good, that you don't need to do the Morning Mindset anymore. But the reality is, it's the Morning Mindset that's causing that feeling. It's so empowering and easy that you may think, "I've got this down. I'm good, I'm on track." You'll be tempted to think you don't really need to keep doing this practice, almost as if the purpose was to just get you on track. But it's not. The purpose is to *keep* you on track and proactively create your day every day for the rest of your life! This is not a one-time prescription that cures you, it's an ongoing daily habit that keeps you aware and growing. Think about the last committed, loving relationship you created. You didn't start that relationship with another person by just getting to know them for a week or two. You kept investing time, nurturing that relationship so it continued to grow and flourish. You had new epiphanies about the relationship as time went on, and you adjusted your expectations and intentions. The same concept applies here. Keep building that relationship with yourself every morning.

Also, the Morning Mindset outcome is unique for everyone. You can't compare what happens to one person with your experience. What areas you need to strengthen are different from the next person, and what you need most will be unique to you. If you struggle with commitment and following through, you'll probably see your initial growth in the intentions and reflection sections. In comparison, the person lacking confidence and trust will likely thrive from affirmations and prayers. We all have our own timing, and trusting you'll get what you need at the right time is part of the journey. What I can say with confidence is that if you're consistent and continue to show up for yourself, your life will change. You'll one day share with me a new perspective and leveling-up that you never expected.

The Morning Mindset is a flourishing relationship that's continuously serving up new awareness and opportunities.

This consistent practice teaches you to create great habits and break bad ones. We can get pulled back to old thinking patterns because, even though they're not aligned with who we're becoming, they're familiar. Changing years of subconscious habits and beliefs is not an easy task. If you recall, we talked about being aware in Chapter Three. You're going to need to lean on your ability to use your conscious mind to execute this practice every morning. If you're like the majority of people, you've spent years waking up and tending to others' needs first. You're wired to see what people need from you, and your day is based on what other people need. It's going to take reprogramming to be successful long term. In the beginning, you'll have success, but when chaos comes, old habits die hard, and you'll be tempted to default back to your old ways and skip out on yourself or trick yourself into thinking you'll do it later. The Morning Mindset will keep you grounded.

When I first started this practice, I chose a new morning thought that would lead to actions more aligned with my new way of thinking versus the default action I was used to: grabbing the phone and checking it. I repeated my thought, "Coffee and God," over and over again as I got out of bed and walked to the coffee maker and my Morning Mindset journal. Coffee and God, coffee and God. That mantra was what got me started! I got coffee and prayed in my Morning Mindset practice, and those were my priorities. I kept repeating it to ensure I wouldn't let my subconscious mind take over and lead me back to old habits. I'm telling you this now so you can set yourself up for success by choosing your mantra.

What will you say to yourself that will lead you straight to your Morning Mindset, starting with yourself?

Some examples from my clients are:

- I choose myself.
- I create my day.
- I'm committed to myself and my success.
- I'm creating my best life first.

You are 100 percent strong enough to make the best choice, and I can promise you that the world won't fall apart if you take ten minutes for yourself first.

Now that you're showing up each morning and working out the questions of the Morning Mindset, you'll start to feel empowered. You'll gain consistency because you're taking action daily. You'll become committed because you're showing up for yourself every day, accomplishing the intentions you set for yourself. You'll be responsible because you're creating what you want to show up in your day. You'll be honest because you're truly assessing how you feel and are aware through reflection on your follow-through and what you allowed to get in the way. You'll be proactive because you're doing this practice before any other demands, and present because you're sitting with yourself and tuning in distraction-free. You won't dwell on feelings of exhaustion or lack of faith, you'll have affirmations and mantras that are all yours to get you back on track.

Even on days when you're lacking follow-through or the energy to succeed, or if you feel like you've been distracted from the Morning Mindset, this practice will continue to keep you on course just by doing it habitually.

It's the simplest, hardest action
you need to take every day.

Sign me up, right?! Who wouldn't want everything I'm describing? Everyone wants it, but not everyone is willing to do the work for it. By "work," I mean looking inward and creating that relationship with yourself. The pen-to-paper work is ten or fifteen minutes, easy. The discipline and commitment are a little more challenging. The awareness, truth, and responsibility are where it gets difficult. You can't unknow what you've learned, that integrity keeps knocking when it knows you're there. I would argue that the majority of people prefer to live in the "ignorance is bliss" state of mind. It feels easier, but I guarantee you it's limiting when it comes to joy and success. This practice is going to give you clarity around pieces of your life that need to change to bring you out of the default life and into your best life. Those changes are going to take work, but it'll be the most rewarding work you do. It's the simplest, hardest action you need to take every day.

Let's look at some milestones to expect with the Morning Mindset:

Seven Days

It's an ongoing daily habit that keeps
you aware and growing.

After practicing the Morning Mindset for a week, you'll feel more in control of your day. You'll experience a different flow because you've set the pace by sitting with yourself and thinking through how you want your day to unfold. You aren't reacting to what everyone else needs from you, so the day feels calmer. Your actions feel intentional because they're premeditated. Your day is happening because you wanted it to, not because it was a surprise chance.

I recently texted my client Renee, who just started the practice a week ago, asking how the Morning Mindset was going.

"Thanks for checking in. This has been by far my BEST week! Mentally and productively! Thank you!!!"

I replied, "Great! You will be tempted to deviate, but stay the course."

"Thank you! It's easy to do, but for some reason hard at the same time."

"Yes, I know. Don't fall victim to stopping."

The "hard" she's referring to is the new habit she's creating. Any new habit is hard. Think back to the last habit you tried to create—getting up early, drinking more water, exercising daily, eating healthy, spending less money—all difficult. You're reprogramming your brain, and usually undoing a bad habit, so it's going to take conscious awareness to not revert back. Even if we know a bad habit doesn't serve us, it's still comfortable and takes time to replace it with a better choice. Just a week in, people feel like they're conquering the world, all because they're starting their day with their own agenda and accomplishing something for themselves before they've done anything for anyone else. There's a great deal of satisfaction that comes from serving yourself and accomplishing an action with intention. You're telling yourself that you matter. Your answers and thoughts may not be deep at the moment, but the commitment to yourself is there, and that packs a powerful punch! You'll see that you're no longer overwhelmed by how to untangle yourself from a day that doesn't start as your own. You're doing the Morning Mindset for *yourself*. Just remember that you feel this way because you're doing the practice daily, not because you've fixed something and can go back to your old ways.

Fourteen Days

Your newfound awareness will bring you into integrity.

Anyone can pretty much sustain a habit for a week, but two weeks is another level of commitment that can push you closer to doing this practice with yourself for a lifetime. By week two, your awareness is going to be in full swing. You've spent two weeks creating awareness around how you feel, what you're affirming, what you're creating, and what you're grateful for. You want this! That awareness is the first step to change and growth. In the default life, your subconscious made most of the decisions, so you weren't tapping into all your resources. But now you're using your conscious mind more than you have before. I will warn you, though, that you'll become painfully aware of the pieces of your life that frustrate you. Understand that there's no bad awareness here, just information to create change. Don't judge yourself for what you're becoming aware of. If you beat yourself up, you won't want to continue to create awareness. People's commitments are tested here. There will be a fork in the road, are you willing to continue creating awareness to step up and make the change, or will you go back to "ignorance is bliss?" The old you will want to choose the latter, but I'm asking you to let the new you make the choice. It's important to remember that, although you're only two weeks into this practice, you're already not the same person you were. The new you is capable of stepping up. You're equipped with different tools: a set of values, a new mind, authenticity, and self-trust. Stay the course. Your newfound awareness will bring you into integrity if you let it.

Two weeks into the Morning Mindset, many of my clients experience a lack of integrity in their actions. They see that they weren't showing up for what they put down as intentions and are making excuses. Their actions aren't matching their affirmations. When they circle back (we cover the Daily Reflection in the next chapter), they see where they lacked integrity in how they were approaching their life. They made those intentions but then got in their own way. Accountability to self is non-negotiable for success. It's awareness and accountability that allow for change and integrity to show up.

Two weeks into the Morning Mindset, I've been seeing more of what's going on around me, and I'm more focused on family time. I've stopped using the iPad as a babysitter for my kid. It's like I've known it for a while and hadn't done anything about it, and that didn't feel good. (Jake, dad and business owner)

I can tell when clients fall off their Morning Mindset after two weeks. I start to hear these kinds of complaints in coaching:

"I'm just off. I'm stressed out and problems are popping up everywhere."

"I don't have enough time in the day, I can't get everything done."

"I'm short-tempered and feel like everything is annoying me."

Due to understanding awareness, intentions, honesty, and responsibility, before I can even say anything, they course-correct themselves. They realize they need to get back to starting the day with themselves.

Problems do not magically disappear with the Morning Mindset. Bad days still come, but they're fewer and become manageable when you build consistency with the practice. When you start your day proactively, you're in a position to deal with situations, conflicts, and decisions as they arise, instead of being reactive and on the defensive because you feel like your life is on a tenuous tightrope.

To stay committed to this practice, you need to be aware of what you're getting from it. Be proactive about tracking your progress. When you experience the Morning Mindset working, keep doing it. Don't let your ego trick you into believing you don't need to. You do.

Thirty Days

You're learning where your opportunities for growth are and taking action.

A month into the Morning Mindset, you're finding your stride. Maybe you've missed a day or two, but you've come a long way in creating this beneficial habit. The results you get for showing up for yourself every morning are gaining momentum. No doubt, you're still enjoying the feeling of pride for the commitment you're keeping. The peace and control in your day have become the norm. That painful awareness you once winced at is now your ally and being put to good use. Your daily awareness has been guiding you to choose desirable intentions and affirmations around what you want to accomplish and who you want to be. If you've been diligent about your practice, those intentions and affirmations you've been setting every day are starting to gain traction.

I've accomplished more in the last thirty days than I can remember doing in months. I finally know how to figure out when something is getting in my way! (Maggie A)

When you put in the work for a month, change happens, and you won't be the only one to see it. If you recall, at the beginning of the book, I promised you that taking time to work on yourself was not a selfish act, and that you would be creating a better version of yourself that would show up even better for others. This is the time you'll see it starting to happen. The change you experience won't be just for you, people around you will notice you're living in a smarter, happier way too. A month in, your values also start to become non-negotiable.

I had a victory call from a client named Rebecca who was thirty days into the practice:

I had someone on my team quit the other day. She left feedback about me in her exit interview. She commented on my leadership skills and specifically referred to my honesty and transparency.

I've been setting intentions around those pieces for weeks. I've been writing affirmations around the leader I am. I know I've been doing the work, but it was really neat to see someone else affirm it. Literally, the exact intentions and affirmations I have been setting are what people around me are seeing. It's working!

When you get to the point where you're really leaning in, it almost feels like a treasure hunt. You're putting some serious thought into your practice and looking for those gems of awareness and opportunity. You're learning where your opportunities for growth are and taking action. You start to see what deeper gratitude feels like, you're more appreciative, and you can even be grateful for a circumstance that didn't work out in your favor. You're going below the surface and getting to know yourself. Self-confidence grows simply because you're getting to know who you are. There isn't less work, but you feel less overwhelmed because you believe in your abilities to manage what you can control and let go of what you can't. You're more in control of your day and what you want out of it. You're reflecting on what has occurred in your day and expanding on the joy and what served you best. You're taking responsibility for what you want to create! You're living an abundant, authentic life full of integrity!

The goal is to be so firm in your practice that even an event or problem that could set you off course won't make you lose your sanity for the day. The practice isn't always perfect. You'll miss a day, or maybe a few, but you'll get back to it. Don't beat yourself up; take responsibility, give yourself grace, and show up tomorrow morning. Can you do it midday if you forget? Of course you can. It can serve as a great reset, but ideally, you want to create from a fresh, clear mind before anything else has a say in your day. People always ask me if I do my Morning Mindset on vacation. The answer is yes. I still want a say in my day. I won't be setting intentions around work, but I still want to connect with myself. I still want to be grateful and be in prayer. Why wouldn't I? The Morning Mindset is something I get to do, not have to do.

Regardless of the swirl around you, the present space for your Morning Mindset is paramount. Increase your odds of success by making time even when you're pulled back to the old place of distraction and people-pleasing. Lean into affirmations that will empower you and remind you of your choice to start with yourself. I have a client that says, "I am creating success, I am creating success," over and over again. Do whatever works for you, but don't leave it to chance. Decide on an affirmation for the sticky days that you can lean on when you have the urge to go back to your old ways.

One Hundred Days

The result is drastic, but the change feels natural.

By now, the Morning Mindset is a way of life. It's as habitual as brushing your teeth. If you don't do it, you feel icky. It's a non-negotiable start to the day. This is how you create your day. You've been showing up for yourself for one hundred days. That's one hundred mornings of awareness about *yourself* before anyone else. You've completed an entire Morning Mindset journal, and it's full of the days you took responsibility for awareness, discernment, and building your life. You start to see how a say in your day on a daily basis is beneficial, not just for yourself, but for the people you work with, your family and friends, and people around you in general. You don't have any intention of going backward and just taking the day you get without your input. By this time, your relationship with yourself is one based firmly on your values. It's full of trust, and it's one you respect. Your authentic self is starting to realize that you don't need to use old behaviors to make things happen. No more judgment, passive-aggressive comments, knee-jerk reactions, or manipulation. Your authentic self is more than capable, and a hundred times more peaceful. You're so aware and present that you catch anything that shouldn't be present, like victim mentality or trying to control your uncontrollable variables. Your Morning Mindset practice has made you your best guide! You're fully in the driver's seat. The result is drastic, but the change feels natural. That natural feeling comes from becoming your authentic self. This happens when you get to know yourself day after day for one hundred days!

Life and business feel easier. I feel like I'm finally showing up as myself, and it's not work anymore. (Todd K)

You live a better life after filling a Morning Mindset journal every day for one hundred days. There is a joy and contentment that comes with every day. You literally become a better version of yourself. You're authentic, live in integrity, and create what you want. If you would like to brush up on what being authentic means, return to Chapter Six and review. See how you're more capable than you've ever been before. No more second-guessing your abilities and what you could do. You envision, believe, and take action. If you've ever had that feeling that you were capable of more, you finally get to find out, because now that you've shown up for yourself every morning and built this relationship, you've never been in a better position to find out what you can really do.

One Year

After three hundred sixty-five days of the Morning Mindset, you'll be living life differently.

You'll have filled up three journals, which are evidence of your commitment to change. To achieve a new life was simple—you left behind what wasn't working for you and changed where you needed it most. Because you're starting the day with yourself consistently, you're confident to create meaningful success and a life you love. You have space away from mental chatter and everything opens up. You have greater bandwidth, and your life is quieter and more serene. You've never felt so abundant. Hello to a limitless mindset and goodbye to the limitations you were dealing with before. Your capability has no limits. This is where it opens up, and what you get varies from person to person.

I asked a few Morning Mindset believers what a year in the practice did for them:

- *"I was grateful for my life before, but now I love it. There is real joy and excitement!"*
- *"Life feels easy and stress-free, I'm not always worrying about everything."*
- *"I get more done in my days in less time than I ever have before."*
- *"The Morning Mindset has shown me where I'm stumbling, and I don't make the same mistakes anymore."*
- *"My mind is so peaceful and clear. I feel like I get to be present in everything I do."*
- *"I feel like I have it all under control instead of feeling like a hot mess all the time."*
- *"I love that it makes me see things I would have never seen if I hadn't asked myself the questions."*
- *"It's given me the time for myself that I learned I deserve."*

The final piece to building this limitless space and staying accountable to how you're growing is in the Daily Reflection. This reflection process keeps you in a circle of motion with yourself. It's a personal recalibration and not a step to be missed. You'll learn where you didn't stand up for your values, neglected your intentions, or were spotty with your gratitude. You'll also celebrate the wins and joys of standing in your new place of power.

10

DAILY REFLECTION

With the Morning Mindset, every morning for a few minutes after you wake, you're practicing awareness, adjusting, setting intentions, saying affirmations, visualizing, and offering gratitude and prayer. It's empowering and feels good to focus on yourself and your mind for the day. The final key element to the practice is Daily Reflection. With Daily Reflection, we book-end the Morning Mindset with an assessment of our day, allowing for observation, celebration, learning, and change. Your Daily Reflection becomes your self-coaching tool, ensuring what you lock into your subconscious you can bring forward into your next day. You took the time to set your day up the way you wanted to, now it's time to check in and reflect. How did you do?

When you do your Daily Reflection is going to depend on when it serves you best. When I originally developed the Morning Mindset, the reflection was intended to be at the end of the day as a way to review and close the door to the day. For those who have a hard time winding down or feel like they can't turn off work, doing the reflection in the evening can create the acknowledgment you need to bring peace to your evening. For myself and some clients, we've found that the reflection was more helpful in the morning right before starting the new Morning Mindset for the day, as it helps to have the reflection fresh in mind when I create the new day. You've heard me say from the beginning of this book that you are your best guide, so remember that mantra when you decide when to do your Daily Reflection. Try the evening and then try the morning. Observe what makes a bigger impact and when you feel more connected to it. Trust yourself, you'll know.

This reflection process is vital for the recalibration of self and growth. How do you grow if you don't know? You'll repeat the same behaviors you did yesterday if you don't know how they happened. I'll hear from a client that they aren't making progress on an area of growth and the first question I ask is, "Are you accomplishing your intentions?" When they don't know if they have, or when the answer is sometimes, it's a red flag that they're bypassing the Daily Reflection. While it's wonderful to consistently do the Morning Mindset, it's imperative that you're accountable to yourself in reflection. Change comes with an honest self-evaluation of your progress.

Part of working toward optimal results is measuring your efforts and making adjustments. You might be familiar with this practice if you've had a review from an employer. You assess how you've been doing to decide where you can improve, just as a business looks at profit and loss to assess where they need to adjust. Without reflection and awareness, how do you know where to change and improve? What I'm going to show you with the Daily Reflection can be universally used in any area of your life. This reflection process keeps you accountable, which is one of the top reasons people work with a coach. Also, it keeps your awareness and intentions new and exciting and it creates a resourceful mind. Your awareness that you're repeating a failing behavior ensures that you don't keep repeating the same actions every day, banging your head against a wall, wondering, "Why is this happening?" Knowledge is power, so you're getting power every time you reflect and gain insight into the course of your day.

You might be tempted to skip this step, thinking, "Isn't the Morning Mindset enough?" Trust me on this, the few minutes it takes you is easy work. It's rewarding because you get to replay the joy and wins that you often miss in the rush of the day. Its accountability gets you to your destination more effectively and efficiently, and you gain knowledge from your experiences. If you could trade two or three minutes to avoid a mistake you made yesterday, wouldn't you?

Don't be tough on yourself if the Daily Reflection shows you're falling short in an area. There's no grade or punishment; there's nothing to be ashamed of or disappointed about. You have to treat this clarity as a gift, not a judgment. This awareness is an opportunity to be your best and live your best life. Gently, day by day and with consistency, you can learn what gets in the way of you following through with your intentions or living your values. Initially, you may struggle to identify areas where you found joy or feel like a victim of what got in the way. In time, that all changes. You'll welcome the knowledge to know what got in the way and take ownership of it instead of being a victim. You'll also find the joy that was there all along, waiting to be seen, and new joy in unexpected areas. The obstacles that were once a mystery, like procrastination, are revealed so you don't hit them again. You uncover joy and wins that bring a smile to your face and inspire you to set your next day up to find more. The celebrations and adjustments feel so good that you can't wait to look at your day to acknowledge the life you're creating! You are your best accountability partner with the Daily Reflection. Let's look at the questions of the daily reflection component of the Morning Mindset in greater detail.

DAILY REFLECTION

Did my values show up?   Did I accomplish my intentions?
☐ Yes ☐ No   ☐ Yes ☐ No

What brought me joy? _____

_____

What was my win? _____

_____

What got in the way? _____

_____

What did I learn? _____

_____

Did Your Values Show Up?

As we discussed in Chapter Two, your values are the core foundation of your well-being. In the Morning Mindset journal, I gave you a place to list your values in the front. Since I'm also a student of my own practice, my values are listed in the front of my journal as:

- Challenge
- Spirituality
- Family
- Alone time
- Feeling competent and capable
- Physiological growth
- Accomplishment
- High Moral Standards

This simple, reflective question, "Did my values show up?" ensures you're staying proactive about living a value-aligned life. When you're rigorously accountable to daily reflection on your values, you find that they've fueled you with energy and joy. They signify what fills your cup every day so you have your best to give. Think of your values as your gas gauge; you want to know when you're running low, and you don't want to just run out of gas. Without this check-in, you would eventually find out if your values were missing, but by then you'd be running on empty. I want you to know before you get discouraged and confused.

It's easy to look at your values daily to bring them into your day, and cross-check them in the Daily Reflection to make sure you're keeping your integrity to them. If you don't plan on using the Morning Mindset journal, get an index card or sticky note and write your values on it. Put it somewhere you can easily see it when you do your Morning Mindset and Daily Reflection. I'm so in-tune with myself from doing the Morning Mindset that I can feel when I haven't gotten my values in. If I feel off, I can look at my list and see exactly what didn't show up. As you start your Daily Reflection, use your list and ask yourself, "Did my values show up?" If the answer is no, you've got an opportunity to be more intentional about it tomorrow.

It's important to check on these for a few reasons. First, it's easy to begin letting these slip and then you find yourself feeling unmotivated or stuck from not fueling up. If you take a proactive approach, you have your finger on the pulse to make sure you're getting what you need. It also creates awareness around *how* they showed up. You might learn something about your values and another way you can meet them. You might also find out that a value has changed because you've changed. Bottom line: keep your eye on what's most important to you!

The Daily Reflection has been super helpful in getting my values to show up every day. I know it sounds silly, but because I know I have to answer that question at the end of the day, I really make sure I get them in so I'm going to be able to say yes! At first, it was a winning thing, like I wanted to be able to say yes, that they showed up. But now I see the real value. I can't believe how much better my day is when I get my values in. My motivation, in the beginning, was to achieve the yes, but now it's changed to filling me up. (Kelley S)

Did You Accomplish Your Intentions?

The next reflection is around your intentions. You set intentions in the Morning Mindset for a reason. Don't mess around with this question or make excuses. This is a simple yes or no. You want to have a say in the actions you're taking during the day. You've chosen those actions for several reasons, including to get your values to show up, take steps to reach a goal, or show up as the best you. Regardless of your reasons, you chose the actions, and you want to make sure you're staying committed and following through with what you decided to accomplish. We talked about building trust with ourselves in Chapter Seven, so here's your chance. When you follow through with your intentions, you build trust. When you don't follow through, but you figure out why, you build trust. It's a win-win. Without follow-through and accountability, you're leaving your results to chance. To be confident in your abilities and achieve what you want, you have to believe you'll act on your intentions.

In the past, you let yourself slide and thought, "I'll do it tomorrow," but it never gets done. Your repeated behaviors formed a story and created subconscious beliefs that didn't serve you. So you gave up, thought *it's not important*, and started to feel unhappy or unmotivated. You have to be able to call yourself out to create awareness and growth. The best way to call yourself out is daily and consistently. That's the only way you'll see a pattern. Morning Mindset users will ask me, "Can't we have a middle box that says 'kind of?'" This tells me they're looking at the question as a performance-based question instead of a growth opportunity. This isn't to shame you, but it's to encourage you to take responsibility and make different choices. I want you to view this reflection on your intentions with gratitude. You get to either celebrate your follow-through or find out what went wrong—there's gratitude for both!

Once I started holding myself accountable for my intentions in the Daily Reflection, they became more important, less like a to-do list. I'm excited to set my intentions and check in on them every evening. I have so much pride in the work I'm doing toward accomplishing my goals. I'm so productive and it feels great. (Carrie K)

What Brought You Joy?

We all want joy in our lives, and it's your responsibility to create or find yours. The day-to-day happenings can make it hard to see the joy or take time to make it, but if you practice asking yourself in your Daily Reflection where you found joy that day, you start to become more aware of what made you joyful and can be more intentional about creating and visualizing it in the morning. You start seeking opportunities to spend time on and focus on those areas that brought you joy. Reflecting on those joyous moments also helps you to relive them and make them grow. When clients reflect on the joy they experienced during their Daily Reflection, they get the added benefit of reliving the feelings again.

We went on a bike ride, sat at the beach, and just took it all in. We were really present. When I wrote that down as a joy, I felt it all over again. It was awesome. (Tara S)

You want to reflect on and capture those moments of joy. Just like you learned in Chapter Four about your mindset, there are times when you aren't fully present in the moment. Reflecting on moments in the evening or the morning after, before you start your Morning Mindset for that day, ensures they don't get overlooked. It can help bring that joy to life again. Tuning in to your daily joy will help you be more present in the moment and start really living those moments and feeling them when they happen. You'll be more conscious of how precious they are. Reflecting on what brought you joy is also an opportunity to learn more about yourself. At some point, you'll likely experience joy in unexpected ways. Discovering those opportunities may lead you to change your values or set intentions to experience this newfound joy.

Where Did You Win?

You experience wins, big and small, all day long, but you may be so busy in the stream of life that you can't see them. You've heard the saying, "Success breeds success." The same theory applies here. Winning breeds winning, but if you don't recognize the wins, it's easy to miss them. Your wins help to increase your confidence and build trust as well. Your win doesn't have to always connect to your list of intentions; there isn't a right or wrong win here. Someone's win might be responding calmly to an angry client, even if this wasn't on their list of intentions that day. It's about you acknowledging yourself for an area you feel like you won in. You're growing every day, that alone presents several opportunities for wins. I hear the statement, "You'd be so proud of me," every week from clients.

"You'd be so proud of me. I said no to something that wasn't that important to me and took the time for myself."

"You'd be so proud of me. I had a client start yelling at me, and instead of being reactive, I took a deep breath and asked him a question."

"You'd be so proud of me. My kids were making me crazy and I chose peace instead of yelling."

Yes, yes, and yes! I am proud, those are your wins! Write them down and celebrate them! Be proud of yourself! We tend to look for acknowledgment and recognition from others when we should be looking to ourselves. Giving yourself credit and acknowledgment for your wins is instrumental in your continued growth. Simply writing them down helps to retain and reinforce them, but you can also go back and read through your wins when you need the encouragement.

Your wins might be something like landing a client, being present, increasing your fees, or ending a toxic relationship. The intentions you set could've been landing a client, living in the moment, making more money, and having a healthy romantic relationship. You decide what your win is. Your win could simply be that you made it through a tough day or that you didn't wake up feeling like your optimal self but pushed through and focused on your intentions anyway. Winning can be overshadowed by all the noise, but when you take a moment to reflect and see where you won, you start to realize that you can persevere. You're stronger than you think, and you're growing and changing. Most people are quick to be hard on themselves, but they rarely take time to celebrate themselves. Find your wins every day and you increase your confidence and build trust with yourself. Both are powerful traits to have when the going gets tough.

What Got In the Way?

Creating awareness around what got in the way of you achieving your intentions and goals is one of the most powerful pieces of the reflection because you can adjust and set yourself up for success! Think back to the last time you said, "Today is the day, I'm going to get this done." Then the end of the day came, and it didn't happen again. You become frustrated, and you start to form thoughts like, "I'm a procrastinator." Maybe you think you just don't want to do something. You lose confidence and trust in yourself, which affects your judgment about your abilities. You become a victim because you aren't taking the time to figure out what's getting in the way. There's a habit, an obstacle, or disconnect that's causing the lack of follow-through. Take an interest in why; be an investigator and figure it out. All you have to do is explore that question: What got in the way? Because you have an honest relationship with yourself, you'll find the answer. You might realize that there was no way, from a time perspective, that you could've accomplished the intention you set, so your expectations were unrealistic. You could've truly forgotten and learned that if you'd put it in your calendar, it would have gotten done, but leaving it to memory is not a good approach. You'll be surprised by the answers you get when you just start asking yourself this in the Daily Reflection. One of my clients uncovered that the intention she was setting was too broad.

I kept setting an intention around creating a marketing plan for the last quarter, but I wasn't following through. Once I asked myself in the Daily Reflection what was getting in the way, I realized I didn't even know where to start with that intention. It's like it was too big to tackle in one intention. (Laura M)

Reflecting on the simple question, "What got in the way?" creates space for growth. When you create your new day, you'll bring forward the lessons learned in your previous reflective time. When you ask what got in the way, you'll be more realistic with your expectations. You'll add that task to your calendar. You'll set a more specific intention that feels approachable. You'll learn from the day before and fine-tune for a different approach the next day. This reflective adjustment allows you to stay curious. That way doubt from the default life doesn't creep in on why you aren't accomplishing what you want. You'll feel more equipped to tackle your bigger, more daunting commitments.

Writing this book while running a successful coaching company and being a partner of an investment firm, wife, and mother was a major undertaking. I didn't have spare time to write. When I didn't write, I had to ask, "What got in the way?" I wasn't putting aside enough time, so I had to create the time. I had to set intentions around the action, write affirmations aligned with my beliefs and abilities, and reflect on what was or wasn't working. It wasn't a perfect journey—my integrity and values were tested—but I had the space to reflect on my intentions daily and make the changes necessary to do better tomorrow. The Daily Reflection created honesty and awareness that eventually got me in the right rhythm, all while keeping my integrity and accomplishing one of my biggest goals. Prior to this daily routine, it would have been left to chance and open to excuses like being too busy, not having enough time, or deciding to try again another day.

What Did You Learn?

You're learning and growing every day, and we want to bring that knowledge to the conscious mind for use. If you don't create awareness around your growth, your subconscious will still pick it up, but there will be a lack of understanding around the growth and what to do with it. It's as if there are missing pieces. When you take the time to ask, "What did I learn today?" you bring that information to the conscious mind, and your brain automatically starts to think about how you can use this information.

Your learning can come from anywhere. It might show up in an inspirational quote, a podcast, a book you're reading, advice from a friend, or your own personal experience in the day. I read at least a few pages a day from a book, and I also read a daily devotional—both great sources of learning for me. Knowing that I'm looking for learning opportunities, I read for growth and knowledge versus completion. This ensures that I'm capturing that gem of information I want to reflect on later. If something gets in the way of your intentions, you have an opportunity to learn there too. What you learn from yourself every day can change your life in drastic ways.

I learned that I'm important and that I need to treat my personal time and appointments with as much respect and commitment as I do my clients. (Beverly G)

While writing this book, in the Daily Reflection, I would ask myself what I learned about the process day to day. I would uncover another opportunity for growth that would bring me closer to dialing in the daily writing habit. I learned that I write best first thing in the morning and that midday never works. I learned that I get in my flow and produce better writing in my home office, so I don't ever plan to write in my business office anymore. Eventually, my subconscious would've told me to stop trying to write in my business office or during midday, but that could've been weeks of frustration and precious time lost. Instead, I proactively created the learning and growth and used it right away.

In Chapters Five and Seven, you learned the importance of taking responsibility to build trust with yourself. Checking in and reflecting is you taking responsibility for what you said you were going to do that day and living in your new level of integrity. From the start of this book, we set the intention for you to live a value-aligned life and follow through with what you intend to create in your day, creating meaningful success (your intentions) and a life you love (your values).

After consistently doing the practice of the Morning Mindset and the Daily Reflection, you've started to function as a different person, you've actually changed. Newfound authenticity and trust show you where you wanted to go originally. You're more capable than you thought you were. You're trusting the authentic part of you alongside the hard work and determination, and what you're seeing is limitless potential. The pieces that used to hold you back, like lack of commitment, lack of confidence, or lack of trust, along with a victim mentality, are no longer an issue because they're not out there untethered and undefined.

You're now creating from a different mind—a limitless mind. There may have been challenges you couldn't conquer before, but you're ready now. You have a system in place to win and a relationship with yourself. What do you really want to create now? Do you want a bigger business? Do you want a new job? Do you want a healthier relationship? Once you see the power behind this potent combination of the Morning Mindset and the Daily Reflection, you're recalibrated to create on a bigger level. You can't help but get better when you create your day, execute your plan, and reflect on growth every single day. You're now in your best life, and the default way doesn't exist anymore. You're in control of creating meaningful success and a life you love!

Embracing the power you hold in this new life will feel so exciting that you might think, "This is it, this is what I've been waiting for." Yes, it's a piece of it, but there's more. Take a breath and acknowledge your growth and power. Now look out and see the blank canvas in front of you. It's time to get inspired to share your greatness!

The Non-Negotiable You

- Reflects daily
- Holds themself accountable
- Looks for growth opportunities

11

INSPIRED YOU

You are capable. You've created a space where you have the ability to tap into your full potential. You're inspired by the new life that has been created by you. You have more capacity than you could ever want. You're energized and motivated by the space you've created by choosing yourself and your values. You have control of your mind and are comfortable letting others think and feel the way they want. You live in the present moment, where you find joy and take action. You show up authentically and you trust yourself. You have a relationship with yourself and continue to grow into the best version of yourself every day. You're inspired to achieve anything your new, limitless mind dreams of. Your resources are applied to useful intentions versus managing all the noise in your head. With this new you comes new possibilities and opportunities. You have inspiration emerging that you've never tapped into before.

Through the teachings in Chapters One through Seven and the Morning Mindset, you've recognized this increased capacity and space. Now you need to protect it like the treasure it is. Don't let the practice get stale after the honeymoon period. You've worked too hard to casually give that space away or let something without meaning fill it. When we discussed Chapter Four, I taught you to be the gatekeeper of your mind. The same concept applies here. You have this new, fresh space and capacity, and you're going to be the gatekeeper of it. I want you to use your daily awareness and values to decide what goes into that space.

You'll also notice in creating this space that there's more quiet. That could feel foreign or uncomfortable. You may be tempted to fill the space with unnecessary noise. Fight that desire. When my clients start to quiet the noise and feel the extra space, they often feel the impulse to question their new state of being. They aren't used to having a quiet mind. But day-to-day happenings become efficient and life feels easier. And of course, it does—it has to in order to make room for the leveling up toward what you truly want.

Clients will come to sessions with me in this quieter state and ask:

- "Shouldn't I be a little stressed or worried about something?"
- "Is it bad that I'm not worried about what others think of me?"
- "Shouldn't I be doing something more?"

If you're asking these same questions, the answer is no. You're living your values, which is helping you say yes to a life that fills you up and no to a life that doesn't. More energy, less drain.

My client Lucy suddenly had all this time because she'd been doing the Morning Mindset for six months. During that time, her relationship with herself had evolved a great deal. She was calling out the stories and questioning the negative voices that had her second-guessing and judging. She had quieted down her mind so much so that she was accomplishing what she wanted in her day in half the time she used to.

"This is insane," she confessed to me. "What do I do with all this time? I know I wanted the quiet and peace in my mind, but should I be doing more?"

"This new space is where you will create greatness! Don't be quick to fill it up out of discomfort," I told her. "You've learned how to control your mindset, which has freed up a great deal of mental bandwidth and energy. Trust that the space you've created is there for a reason."

You were at a breaking point before, and now, you're having breakthroughs.

More mental capacity, less overwhelm. More energy physically and mentally, less mental drain. You trust yourself, no more second-guessing. More capacity, less doubt. Everything you've been learning along the way and implementing in your Morning Mindset has gotten you here, to an inspired you. Embrace it. Enjoy it. Now you have more room to invite peace in, create new experiences, and call in new dreams for yourself. The discomfort is a temporary by-product of this experience—it's a natural part of this process. You've given up old behavior that's been a part of you forever. Even though the old behavior wasn't good for you, there will still be an empty space where it was. There's no quick answer here as to what to fill it with. The unknown might make you uncomfortable, but you know how to choose your thoughts to create different feelings. I want you to choose excitement and gratitude for the unknown. This is an exciting opportunity you have, so be grateful and excited about what lies ahead.

Prepare for a shift to occur in your Morning Mindset practice. When you're no longer busy all day trying to keep your head above water and reacting to everything, you can go beyond what you've ever had the bandwidth for in the past. You can actually make time to envision and call in greatness that's aligned with what you've been building in the Morning Mindset. You're ready to tap into what you're truly capable of. You were at a breaking point before, and now you're having breakthroughs. The Morning Mindset that got you to this place is also going to help you discover what you're inspired to tap into. In the beginning, you did the Morning Mindset to create a consistent, committed, and honest relationship with yourself. The goal was to get you to a healthy place with yourself and quiet the noise so you could lead yourself well. You're there now, and you have the opportunity to expand the value of your practice to what really inspires you.

You'll know the shift is coming when you start to feel like you're in a steady flow with your practice and your answers are feeling a little routine. Don't judge, you needed those answers in the beginning; they served a purpose. But you've grown, and your Morning Mindset wants to grow with you. So if you become aware that it's getting repetitive, that's your cue to dig a little deeper. Look inward, listen more intently, and wait patiently for the answers that will come from a deeper place. Challenge yourself to find the answers beyond what's been coming up for you. Look at the potential difference in your responses.

For example, when you first started the Morning Mindset, you thought in vague generalities, like, "I feel good." There's nothing wrong with feeling good, you were aiming for that in the beginning. But now you have more space, and if you really want to tap into your greatness, you need to go deeper, beyond the first answer that pops into your mind. What if you explored what's creating the good feeling and uncovered the deeper answer? For example, "I feel excited about inspiring other people."

These are two completely different answers. The "good" is fine, but it's going to lead you down a much different path for the day than the leveled-up answer, "inspired to help others." The first answer might be status quo—keeping you on track and accomplishing what you set out to do—but if you tune in to feeling excited about inspiring others, you might uncover intentions around something new and exciting that you can create to inspire others. Your entire Morning Mindset practice unfolds differently when you come from this deeper awareness, but it's going to require patience. You have it in you, but you're going to have to look for it.

Growth and change happen in uncomfortable moments.

A word of caution: Don't be too quick to jump into the next "best" idea. You're capable of accomplishing many things, so your mind will naturally serve some quick and easy options. Be willing to let them go and pass on them; you can always go back to it later if it feels right! Give yourself some time, there's no need to feel pressured. The old you would be thinking, "What's next? What's next?" If you jump into something too quickly just to fill your time and space, you could be missing what's really meant to be there. I want you to sit with the possibilities and be patient, embracing the space, because something meaningful deserves to fill it. Like I said before, the new space might feel uncomfortable. Take it as a good sign; growth and change happen in uncomfortable moments. If you pause here for a moment, and think about what's in your mind, you'll find glorious empty space. This is your blank canvas to start creating what you want and tapping into what you're capable of. You were born with a gift and a purpose, and it's time to start uncovering it. You might be tested and pulled back into old behaviors in this new space. Stay aware and protect this new opportunity you've created. Just because you have this additional space and time doesn't mean you compromise your values. My client Audrey mentioned that she felt like her Morning Mindset was becoming too routine, like her answers were often the same and weren't creating the spark they did in the beginning. I advised her to go deeper and not take the first answer that comes up. I invited her to challenge herself by asking, "What else?"

"It's finally happening! I'm getting to the next level in the Morning Mindset!" she told me later with excitement.

"So, what did you do?" I inquired.

"I started to write down what came to my mind, and then I remembered what you said about asking, 'What else?' So I crossed it out and asked myself, 'What else?' It was hard because I felt like nothing was coming up, but as I sat there waiting, new thoughts started to creep into my mind. It was weird to think I could choose wants or goals outside of my normal day of work or what I do," she said.

"Okay. Where do you notice a difference?" I asked.

"My intentions seemed like they were new and exciting. If I had other things under my control, why not use this space for something above and beyond what's normal for me? I know I can do my job well and could just do more of it, but why not shoot for something more exciting and challenging? I'm looking at life in a different way. It feels like I have the opportunity to be innovative!"

Just because you have this new capacity and blank canvas doesn't mean you should feel pressured to use it. Getting to this place of peace and opportunity is a big win, and this might be all you want right now. That's okay. You get to marinate in the fact that you're starting with yourself and looking for your best life. You only need to keep this commitment to nurture this relationship with yourself, the rest will come when the time is right. Trust that, trust yourself.

As the inspired you, when a new, exciting idea hits, you're going to have to remember that you're a different person than you were before. You can handle the expansion and growth. Past experiences might make you think that you've tried this before, but that was the old you. You didn't have the capacity or foundation you have now. You're equipped with a whole new set of tools to lean on: your values, awareness, mindset, responsibility, authenticity, trust, plus your Morning Mindset and Daily Reflection. Don't fall victim to letting past experiences control your thoughts about what you can accomplish. I want you to approach your ideas with your new mindset, knowing you're capable of so much more than you were before.

What have you become through this process of the Morning Mindset? A leader in your life. You're now in the best place to lead other people if that's what you choose to do. If you felt like you failed before in an area of your life, you can return to those goals and dreams now in a more authentic way and with a recalibrated thinking process. Give what you thought was dead another try, or decide fully, without reservation, that you never want to do it again. The win for you now is choosing the best life for yourself through authenticity, which can lead you to what you want with newfound clarity.

You're on the path to living your best life for yourself and creating meaningful success. Now you're ready to start setting those big, audacious goals and achieving your wildest dreams. You get to decide where you want to see changes. Where do you want to grow? You're ready to start assessing what changes you want to make in your life. Welcome to this place of discovery!

This book is not a one-time read. It's a user manual to living your best life. You've made great strides, but your growth will be tested. If, at any point, you feel off and are wavering back to the default life, pick up this book. Ask yourself, "What is the challenge for me right now?" Find the relevant chapter and reread it. The knowledge you need will come back to you, getting you back on the right path.

- Are you feeling unmotivated or lost? Read Chapter Two on your values.
- Do you feel like you don't know what to do next? Read Chapter Three about your awareness.
- Is your mind controlling you again? Read Chapter Four on why your mindset matters.
- Are you blaming others or feeling like a victim? Read Chapter Five on taking responsibility.
- Are you showing up as someone you're not? Read Chapter Six to rediscover your authenticity.
- Are you worrying and doubting too much? Read Chapter Seven on trusting yourself.

The Morning Mindset offers self-awareness and coaching that can be implemented at any time so you can course-correct. You never have to go back to the old way of thinking. Don't give up on what's working. You can do the Morning Mindset for the rest of your life. Why would you stop something that's so simple and takes so little time, yet produces so many results?

So what's next? You've created this amazing relationship with yourself and you now feel more confident and capable than ever before. You've ditched the default life, and you're now empowered and responsible for what you're creating and growing. You trust yourself because you know you're organized and focusing on creating your best life in a consistent, value-driven way. You're finally showing up for yourself in the way you deserve. Just keep starting with yourself every day and trust yourself to make it happen.

12

MORNING MINDSET SAMPLES

I have clients who ask me all the time to share my Morning Mindset and Daily Reflection work. I'm always hesitant because there's no one right way that's going to magically make change happen in your life. It's about cultivating a relationship with yourself that you have awareness of and trust in, that's what will make your practice serve you well. I'm trusting you to use your self-awareness to guide yourself. Remember that this is your practice, and as you progress, you'll feel what's right for you.

I do, however, understand the desire to want to do the work correctly and see an example. Therefore, I'm sharing a few sample Morning Mindset entries from different clients at different stages in their practice and mine as well. Each person who has willingly shared their Morning Mindset is on a different growth journey. Be careful not to judge someone else's words, as it will hinder you from being honest with your own. Everyone has different values, goals, dreams, and intentions for their life. View these as examples and not comparisons. Your practice will reflect your authenticity.

Morning Mindset of a CEO, mother of three, and wife:

Awareness

I feel: Fantastic.

Adjustments

I can: Keep true to my routine.

Intentions

I will:

1. Pray throughout the day
2. Compliment others
3. Listen
4. Ask questions
5. Practice presence

Affirmations

I am: Abundant. Limitless. Kind. Helpful and generous. A phenomenal wife and mom. Intentional and focused.

Gratitude

I'm grateful for: Time with my husband. Getting to meet with Angie. Celebrating my daughter's birthday. Being rested. Listening to a great podcast on a great run.

Prayer

I'm asking: Dear God, please help me stay more patient and understanding as a mom. Help me practice control and quietly support others!

Visualization

I see: Us making memories in our dream home with five bedrooms and a pool! I run a hundred-million-dollar company that is changing lives. We own our corporate headquarters and world headquarters.

Daily Reflection

Did my values show up? Yes.

Did I accomplish my intentions? Yes.

What brought me joy? Early run with my friend, my audible book, and coaching my daughter.

What was my win? Staying present on a busy day at the store.

What got in the way? Talking more than practicing silence, active listening.

What did I learn? I need to ask more questions.

Morning Mindset of a business owner, father, and husband:

Awareness

I feel: Determined.

Adjustments:

I can: Continue to stay present, inspired, and motivated.

Intentions

I will:

1. Edit one or two items on the shop
2. Finish taxes and talk to my CPA
3. Ship completed orders
4. Be present
5. Stay motivated

Affirmations

I am: At peace. I am calm. I am abundant. I am present. I am healthy. I am blessed. I am grateful. I am wealthy. I am focused. I am inspired. I am the shit. I am a warrior. I am a rockstar. I am unique. I am living my best life. I am confident. I am amazing. I am a magnet for money and business. I am a badass. I am limitless.

Gratitude

I'm grateful for: A powerful group coaching session. To spend time with family in the morning. My new marketing team. Joseph helping me out with office decoration. Feeling like I have a better grip on life. Wife cooking for me.

Prayer

I'm asking: For a peaceful, strong, focused, and inspired mindset. Health for my family, friends, and myself. Constant influx of money and business. More awareness to be a better leader and an example to my son.

Visualization

I see: Myself being very successful in business, very wealthy, healthy, and with my family by my side.

Daily Reflection

Did my values show up? Yes.

Did I accomplish my intentions? Yes.

What brought me joy? Seeing friends and family for a drink in the evening.

What was my win? I ended a full week of focused, intentional work, and it feels so good!

What got in the way? I got a bit anxious at the place where I met friends. There were a lot of people and I started to sweat.

What did I learn? That I deserve as much money as I want.

**Morning Mindset of a real estate agent,
team leader, husband, and father:**

Awareness

I feel: Confident.

Adjustments

I can: Pray and talk to God.

Intentions

I will:

1. Follow up with Juanita
2. Follow up with Raul
3. Call for one hour
4. Follow up on supers
5. Eat healthy

Affirmations

I am: Confident. Consistent in all areas of my life. Earning $600,000 in 2022. Systematic in my business. Glorifying God in everything I do.

Gratitude

I'm grateful for: God. My church. My wife. My kids. Fab Five. Health. Our home. Our neighborhood. Savings. Food. My iPad. Big bear. My clients. My business. Opportunities. Work. Family.

Prayer

I'm asking: God, according to his will, to help close Big Bear smoothly in March. To help close E.'s escrows smoothly and on time. To help me be consistent in prospecting in March. To list two houses above one million in March. To help get J. in escrow in March. To help me share the gospel with my brother.

Visualization

I see: Myself achieving all my goals while keeping God above all.

Daily Reflection

Did my values show up? Yes.

Did I accomplish my intentions? Yes.

What brought me joy? Feeling worthy and confident.
What was my win? Following through with my prospecting.

What got in the way? Nothing.

What did I learn? I'm capable of accomplishing anything I want.

Morning Mindset of an entrepreneur:

Awareness

I feel: Rested but sore. Ready for the day.

Adjustments

I can: Allow myself grace as I tackle my commitments.

Intentions

I will:

1. Stay in the present moment.
2. Practice gratitude.
3. Make a to-do list and focus on each task.
4. Nourish myself and take breaks.
5. Talk less, listen more.

Affirmations

I am: Worthy of love, joy, and compassion. Abundance flows to me easily and effortlessly. I am grateful for what I have now, knowing more abundance is on its way.

Gratitude

I'm grateful for: My body and its ability to get up. My husband, dog, and parents. Increased intuition and awareness. Having things I once dreamed of. My business that allows me to be creative and serve others.

Prayer

I'm asking for: Additional abundance in family and finance. Increasing my monthly income $20,000 more, and this beautiful and healthy pregnancy. Ways to chase my dreams and live my service.

Visualization

I see: Myself promoting my company. Traveling to India, UK, and Germany.

Daily Reflection

Did my values show up? Yes.

Did I accomplish my intentions? Yes.

What brought me joy? The feeling of accomplishment at the end of the day.

What was my win? Project movement from positive pressure.

What got in the way? Feeling full moon in Cancer, Mercury retrograde.

What did I learn? I'm stronger than I know

Morning Mindset Progression

Here is an example of the progression of one person's Morning Mindset from the beginning, to thirty days in, sixty days in, and then ninety days in. You can see how it evolves as the relationship with themselves develops.

Day 1

Awareness

I feel: Like I don't want to work. I don't know, unmotivated and kind of stuck.

Adjustments

I can: Have a good podcast. Do some prayer. Stay off social. Remember that my "why" is to help other people.

Intentions

I will:

1. Workout
2. Plan my week
3. Get tax info uploaded
4. Start this week strong
5. Think positively

Affirmations

I am: Building a life I love that honors God. Strong, courageous, and capable. At peace in the present and finding joy in the moment. Attracting the right clients.

Gratitude

I'm grateful for: Early mornings. A strong client roster. A team who can help. New opportunities. Making my own schedule. A new week. My dog and everything she teaches me. My mom's love and support. The time to finish a painting.

Prayer

I'm asking for: Strength, provision, and protection over my partner and our families. Enough joy and patience and energy to get me through today. Salvation for my mom and dad. Guidance in growing my business. Healing for those who are sick and hurting. Enough for today!

Visualization

I see: Myself showing up today, shaking off this heaviness, and kicking today's butt.

Daily Reflection

Did my values show up? Yes.

Did I accomplish my intentions? Yes.

What brought me joy? Getting things done.

What was my win? Painting.

What got in the way? The day didn't start the best, but I got on track! Thank you, Lord.

What did I learn? You can turn your day around.

60 days

Awareness

I feel: Better. Ready to make this a great week.

Adjustments

I can: Stay focused on one task at a time.

Intentions

I will:

1. Accomplish my to-do list
2. Be present
3. Have fun
4. Finish Bible study
5. Paint

Affirmations

I am: In control of my thoughts. At peace in the present. Building a life that I love that honors God. Strong, courageous, and capable.

Gratitude

I'm grateful for: My clients and my team. A full day of items to accomplish. Provision, that I have all that I need. My salvation and help from the Holy Spirit. The ability to be flexible and helpful.

Prayer

I'm asking for: Strength, provision, and protection over my partner and our families. Enough of everything I need for today. Guidance in growing my business and cultivating a healthy marriage. Salvation for my parents. Full-term pregnancies for M., L., and M.

Visualization

I see: Myself showing up with the energy and focus I need for today. A productive day!

Daily Reflection

Did my values show up? Yes.

Did I accomplish my intentions? No.

What brought me joy? Hanging with mom.

What was my win? Completing task list.

What got in the way? My task list took longer than I had expected.

What did I learn? Be more realistic about how much time a task will take.

90 days

Awareness

I feel: Good! Really good!

Adjustments

I can: Stay off my phone. Podcast. Coffee. Walk.

Intentions

I will:

1. Have a good Monday
2. Lead my team
3. Finish my task list
4. Find joy in every moment

Affirmations

I am: Strong, courageous, and capable. Building a life that I love and that honors God. Attracting an abundant life. In control of my thoughts.

Gratitude

I'm grateful for: Sobriety (yesterday, I really wanted to drink or smoke). The opportunity to help my clients. New opportunities and financial abundance. A relationship that pushes me to grow. Salvation. My mom. Our home.

Prayer

I'm asking for: Provision, strength, and protection over D.S. and our families. Guidance in growing my business and becoming a good wife. Salvation for my dad. Guidance for mom. Favor over my team, clients, and new team members who are committed to the vision.

Visualization

I see: A happy and healthy marriage. A growing seven-figure business. Sold-out collections.

Daily Reflection

Did my values show up? Yes.

Did I accomplish my intentions? Yes.

What brought me joy? Being able to help people.

What was my win? Painting!

What got in the way? Nothing.

What did I learn? I can have it all.

Morning Mindset of a CFO, coach, mother of two, and wife:

As promised, now I'll share my own personal Morning Mindset. I'm a student as much as I'm a teacher. Every day when I wake up, I do my Morning Mindset. Here's mine from yesterday:

Awareness

I feel: Excited about the ideas that are brewing.

Adjustments

I can: Stay focused and prioritize.

Intentions

I will:

1. Stay in the present moment.
2. Write the outline for challenge content.
3. Put my phone away after work.
4. Spend one-on-one time with my sons.
5. Take time to get outside.

Affirmations

I am: I am a child of God. I am authentic. I am patient. I am a connector and relationship-builder. I am present. I am organized. I am healthy. I am full of energy. I live in abundance. I am a best-selling author. I am a path-creator.

Gratitude

I'm grateful for: Thank you for the beautiful sunrise. Thank you for the family dinner full of laughter and connection. Thank you for the opportunity to use my gifts to help other people. Thank you for keeping my family healthy. Thank you for the huge smile and laughter I saw in my son. Thank you for the support from my husband. Thank you for blessing my business with growth and abundance.

Prayer

I'm asking for: I pray you light my path. I pray you keep my son safe in his travels this weekend. I pray you give Michelle strength and courage to advocate for herself. I pray you put people in my path that I can help. I pray you give me words to speak and write that will inspire others. I pray you help Erin find her joy and choose herself.

Visualization

I see: A productive day, focusing on the moment I'm in. I see connected family time full of love and laughter. I see myself signing books and celebrating it being a best-seller.

Daily Reflection

Did my values show up? Yes.

Did I accomplish my intentions? Yes.

What brought me joy? Having time freedom in my day to do a few things for myself.

What was my win? Getting the office organized.

What got in the way? Nothing.

What did I learn? I learned that I need more time buffers in between tasks to allow for realistic expectations.

Now it's your turn. Start your Morning Mindset now and give yourself the gift of living your best life and creating meaningful success. You deserve it.

ABOUT THE AUTHOR

As a Master Certified Coach and co-owner of alternative investment firm Wisdom Trading Inc., Angie possesses the ability to view and solve high-level problems with a nuanced approach. She has helped countless business owners elevate themselves and their companies by implementing actionable systems that tap into their full potential and put their development at the top of their own priority list. Her Master Coaching Certification places Angie in the esteemed 4% of the coaches in the country with an MCC designation.

A speaker and author, she has graced stages nationwide, sharing "The Morning Mindset" method with thousands. Angie is a member of The Female Founder Collective, Executive Coaches of Orange County, International Coaching Federation, and a contributor to The Forbes Coaching Council. In addition to writing, speaking and inspiring change, she loves to golf, dive and hike with her family. Angie currently resides in Newport Beach, California, with her husband, two boys, and two dogs.

Made in the USA
Monee, IL
26 October 2024

2e5970d7-2ec9-4540-a918-75ca76cb05d4R01